WHICH GCSEs?

THE ESSENTIAL GUIDE TO CHOOSING GCSES

ALISON DIXON

HONEYMAN
PUBLISHING

Which GCSEs? The essential guide to choosing GCSEs

First edition

Published by Honeyman Publishing 2020
honeymanpublishing@gmail.com

© Alison Dixon
www.alisondixon.co.uk

ISBN 978-0-244-45264-3

Please note that all the information in this publication was correct at the time of writing.

Cover design and typesetting by Andy Southan, Big Pond Design.

In memory of

Sue Mairis

1948-2020

A dear friend and an inspirational manager

Acknowledgements

With thanks to Andy Southan, Helen Evans and Stuart Evans.

About the author

Alison Dixon is a qualified careers adviser, careers writer and editor. She started her career in publishing at Penguin Books and then trained as a careers adviser.

After working as a careers adviser in schools and colleges in West and South London, Alison became a careers information specialist and later an operations manager in the career guidance sector. She is now a self-employed careers writer and editor and is the current editor of Career Matters, the membership magazine of the Career Development Institute. She is a Registered Career Development Professional with the Career Development Institute and a member of the Careers Writers Association.

She is the author of *Which A levels?* and she has contributed to *Career Journeys for Young People: a starter guide for parents and carers.*

www.alisondixon.co.uk

CONTENTS

GCSE subjects

HOW GCSES HAVE CHANGED

Between September 2015 and summer 2019, new-style GCSEs were introduced in schools across England.

What's different about the revised GCSEs?

• They include new topics and more demanding content.

• GCSEs used to be made up of modules and students were assessed on each module separately. The revised courses are designed for two-year study and are mainly assessed by final exams at the end of the two-year course.

• Exams are now the main form of assessment so there is far less assessed coursework. The exceptions are subjects like drama, music, design and technology, and art and design, where practical exams and assessment of coursework is necessary; for example through an art portfolio, design project or performance assessment.

• Resit exams in November are now only available in English language and maths, and then only if you get a grade below 4.

• Higher and foundation tier papers are now only available for maths, the sciences and some modern foreign languages.

New grading system

The grading system has changed from A*-G to 9-1, with 9 being the highest grade. There is also a U grade which means ungraded .The Department for Education recognise grade 4 as a standard pass and grade 5 as a strong pass.

If you don't get a grade 4 or above in English and maths you must continue to study them either in full or part-time education or as part of voluntary work, an apprenticeship or job with training.

Higher and lower tiers

Exam papers for the reformed GCSEs in maths, the sciences and some modern foreign languages, including French, German and Spanish are split into foundation and higher tiers. The higher tier papers are targeted at students capable of achieving higher grades, and awards grades from 9 to 4, while foundation tier papers cover grades 5 to 1. Your school or college will advise which tier is suitable for you for those subjects.

GCSE GRADING COMPARISON TABLE

New grading structure	Former grading structure
9 8 7	A* A
6 5 4	B C
3 2 1	D E F G
U	U

GCSEs in Wales and Northern Ireland

GCSEs in Wales have also been reformed:

• Grading scales remain A* to G.

• Some GCSEs will be 'linear' with all exams taken at the end of the course; some will be modular.

• Students must retake all their exams when retaking a linear GCSE; non-exam assessment marks can be reused.

• Students can only retake each module once in modular GCSEs.

Northern Ireland also has reformed GCSEs:

• In general, students may take GCSEs graded A* to G (including a new grade C*) with CCEA and those graded 9 to 1 from the English exam boards.

CHOOSING YOUR GCSES

Your school will give you all the information about subjects available and will ask you to state your choices. There is usually an options evening at school which you can attend with your parents or carers where all the options will be explained and you will be able to ask questions about different courses.

How many do I take?

On average most students take nine subjects. You might combine taking some GCSEs together with other qualifications e.g. Level 2 awards in areas like sport, travel and tourism, hospitality and catering, or information technology, or perhaps the Certificate in Financial Education or Microsoft Office Specialist certification.

When do I choose?

In England, you usually choose the subjects you want to study for GCSE in year 9, but in some schools this might happen in year 8, so even if you're in year 7 it's not too early to start thinking about your options!

How do I choose?

Compulsory subjects

Mathematics, English and science are the core subjects everyone must take at GCSE in England. English language is compulsory in all schools, and so is English literature in the majority of schools, but you need to check what your school expects students to take. If you are at school in Wales, Welsh is compulsory.

Science choices

GCSE science qualifications can be taken in different ways – you can take single GCSEs in one or more of biology, chemistry and physics, or you can take a double GCSE in combined science. Students who take combined science study all three sciences and they'll cover roughly two thirds of the content of the single GCSEs in biology, chemistry and physics.

If you take the single GCSEs, you get a 9 to1 grade for each subject. If you take the combined science qualification, you receive an award worth two GCSEs with two grades, for example, (9-9), (9-8), (8-8) through to (1-1).

Optional subjects

You will have the option to choose:

- **A modern foreign language**. The most commonly taught are French, German and Spanish, but some schools also offer languages like Mandarin Chinese and Russian. Some schools require students to take a modern foreign language, so check whether a language is part of your options or compulsory.

- **A humanities subject** like history, geography or religious studies.

- **An arts subject** like music, drama, art and design or media studies.

- **A technical subject** such as design and technology, food preparation and nutrition or computer science.

- All students have to do **PE** in years 10 and 11, but this could also be taken as a GCSE option.

In most schools, you choose at least one GCSE from each of these categories. Your choice might be restricted, for example by the timetable (e.g. if music is timetabled at the same time as German, you can only take one), or by ability (for example, in some schools, only certain pupils are allowed to take two languages).

Some tips on how to choose

- You need to choose subjects that you enjoy and will do well at.

- You need to keep your options open as not many people have a clear idea of a career path at this stage. So you need to choose options that give you a balanced selection of subjects. (Schools will generally make sure that you do this.)

- Think about where your choices might lead and plan for later on when you will be choosing A levels or equivalent, or applying for apprenticeships or jobs with training.

- You might want to do a subject because your friend wants you to do it or favourite teacher is teaching it. Think carefully about whether this is the right reason for your choice.

- Remember that in the end, the choice is yours – so choose carefully.

English Baccalaureate (or EBacc)

This is not a separate qualification, but a combination of different GCSEs. These are English language and literature, maths, science (GCSE combined science or three subjects from biology, chemistry, physics and computer science), geography or history and a language (which can be ancient or modern).

The EBacc is a performance measure for schools, not a qualification for pupils, and schools are assessed on their performance in these particular GCSEs.

Resits

Students who achieve grade 4 or above in GCSE English language and maths don't need to resit these exams post-16. If you don't get these grades, your college, school or employer (if you are on an apprenticeship) has to provide you with the opportunity to resit these two subjects.

Alternatives to GCSEs

You will see from the table that there are alternatives to GCSEs such at BTECs at Level 1 or 2. You might take a BTEC and a selection of GCSEs. There are also qualifications such as Cambridge Technicals at Level 2 and Functional Skills. You might also be able to take other vocational qualifications such as Certificate in Financial Education at Level 2.

GCSES FOR FURTHER STUDY AND CAREERS

GCSEs are the first rung of an education and training ladder. You can see from the table below that GCSEs are at Levels 1 and 2 and that you can progress on the ladder in full-time education or through an Apprenticeship.

You need to check with your school, future college or sixth form college, for their GCSE requirements to study A levels or equivalent qualifications, such as the BTEC National, Cambridge Technicals or T levels.

Level	Examples of qualifications	Apprenticeships/ training
Level 8	Doctorate e.g. PhD	Masters Apprenticeship
Level 7	Masters, PGCE, Graduate Diploma	Degree or Masters Apprenticeship
Level 6	Degree	Higher or Degree Apprenticeship
Level 5	Foundation degree, HND, DipHE	Higher Apprenticeship
Level 4	Higher National Certificate	Higher Apprenticeship
Level 3	AS and A levels, International Baccalaureate, BTEC Level 3	Advanced Apprenticeship
Level 2	GCSEs (grades 9-4), BTEC Level 2	Apprenticeship
Level 1	GCSEs 3-1, BTEC Level 1	Traineeship
Entry Level	Skills for life, Entry level certificates	

A levels

For further A level study, the usual requirement is a minimum of five or six GCSEs at grade 4 or above, including maths and English. Schools/colleges may also require that a student has a specific grade in the subject(s) they wish to study for A level (or a similar subject if the subject wasn't available at GCSE, for example music technology).

Some schools and colleges offer a mix of A levels and other qualifications such as BTECs and may have different requirements for these courses.

Vocational study

For vocational qualifications such as the BTEC National (an alternative to A levels) the entry requirement is usually a minimum of four GCSEs at grades 9-5, or alternative Level 2 qualifications. You must check with your school or college for their requirements.

Degree-level study

The majority of degree courses require GCSE English language and mathematics at grade 5 or higher, or equivalent qualifications. Some courses may specify grades higher than 5, or additional GCSE passes at certain grades in specific subjects.

GCSEs for careers

English and maths GCSEs at good grades are necessary for entry to many jobs. Competitive careers have higher requirements.

These requirements are only a guide and you must check entrance requirements for each area.

THINKING ABOUT YOUR FUTURE AFTER GCSES

Apprenticeships and traineeships

Traineeships

They help you to develop skills and confidence in the workplace. They can last from six weeks to a maximum of six months and give you extra help and skills so that you can progress to an apprenticeship or further training. You aren't paid for a traineeship but you may be given expenses for things like travel or meals. For more information visit www.gov.uk/find-traineeship

Apprenticeships

Apprenticeships have been popular in countries like Germany and Switzerland for many years and are recognised routes into many professions. In the UK, although a valid and successful route in years gone by, they have taken a while to become established as an alternative to higher education. They are now gaining in popularity as people realise how they can help your career as well as being a cost-effective way of obtaining qualifications, even up to degree level.

Apprenticeships are an alternative to full-time study. Some people find that learning through an apprenticeship suits them as you get real experience of the workplace as well as studying for a qualification and, of course, you are paid as well. You can apply while you are still at school.

Apprenticeships are available in many career areas. They are offered at different levels:

- Intermediate Apprenticeships – equivalent to GCSE level (Level 2)
- Advanced Level Apprenticeships – equivalent to A level or BTEC National (Level 3)
- Higher Apprenticeships – equivalent to a Level 4 qualification or higher (Level 5/6)
- Degree Apprenticeships – equivalent to a Level 6/7 qualification.

For more information, and to search for Apprenticeships, visit www.apprenticeships.gov.uk

Higher Apprenticeships

Higher Apprenticeships are an alternative to full-time higher education as more companies, including major employers such as Rolls Royce, BT and PWC, run these programmes. Apprentices work towards qualifications at higher education level, gain valuable work experience and skills for their CV, and get paid at the same time.

Degree Apprenticeships

These are apprenticeships where study for a degree is an integral part of the programme. Some are available through universities and some through employers.

They are available in many different areas with new ones coming on stream all the time. Examples include accountancy, banking, broadcast and media, business management, engineering and technology of all types, food technology, healthcare, human resources, information technology, nursing, sales, surveying, public relations, police, and science.

For more information on Higher and Degree Apprenticeships visit www.gov.uk/government/publications/higher-and-degree-apprenticeships

Full-time study: A level equivalents

There are a number of other qualifications you might study after GCSEs as an alternative to A levels.

The most common are:

BTEC Nationals

BTEC National qualifications are specialist vocational qualifications useful for entry to employment and higher education. They are practical, work-related courses and are at Level 3, the same level as A levels. They focus on applied knowledge and understanding of a particular area. They are available in many areas including business, construction, health and social care, music technology, performing arts and science. A BTEC National Diploma is equivalent to two A levels and a BTEC National Extended Diploma is equivalent to three A levels. For more information visit www.pearson.com.

T levels

T levels are new courses rolling out from September 2020, and will be equivalent to three A levels. These two-year courses have been developed in collaboration with employers and businesses so the content is relevant to employment and prepares you for work, as well as entry to higher education.

T levels are a mixture of classroom learning and work experience, involving an industry placement of at least 315 hours (approximately 45 days). They can lead to employment, further study or a Higher Apprenticeship.

T levels will be introduced in the following areas:
accountancy; agriculture, land management and production; animal care and management; building services engineering; catering; craft and design; cultural heritage and visitor attractions; design and development; design,

surveying and planning; digital business services; digital production, design and development; digital support and services; education; financial; hair, beauty and aesthetics; health; healthcare science; human resources; legal; maintenance, installation and repair; management and administration; manufacturing, processing and control; media, broadcast and production; onsite construction; science.

For more information visit www.tlevels.gov.uk

Cambridge Technicals

Cambridge Technicals are vocational qualifications and designed for the workplace as well as allowing progression to higher education. The qualifications allow for a high degree of flexibility with the choice of units that make up the qualifications, so you can specialise in the specific areas of the subject that interest you most. Cambridge Technicals are available in many subject areas including art and design, business, digital media, engineering, health and social care, information technology, performing arts, science/applied science, sports and physical activity.

For further information visit www.ocr.org.uk

ANCIENT HISTORY

Are you interested in how the past shapes the way we are today and continues to influence our future? Ancient history GCSE explores the ancient world. You get to study some of the important characters from this period, including Alexander the Great, Cleopatra and Hannibal. It also covers important events such as the Battle of Thermopylae, the foundation of Rome and the creation of democracy.

You study the history and culture of Ancient Greece and Rome including their systems of government, the structure of their societies, their building works and their religious practices.

What you study

The topics listed give a broad idea of what you will study. You will need to check with your school or college for the options available to you.

Greece and Persia

The compulsory period study focuses on the Persian Empire under Cyrus the Great, Cambyses II, Darius I and Xerxes I. You look at the substantial developments and issues associated with this period.

You also study one subject in depth from:

• From Tyranny to Democracy, 546-483 BC

• Athens in the Age of Pericles, 462-429 BC

• Alexander the Great, 356-323 BC.

Rome and its neighbours

The compulsory period study focuses on the kings of Rome and the early Roman Republic, with an emphasis on the most interesting events and characters.

You also study one subject in depth from:

• Hannibal and the Second Punic War, 218-201 BC

• Cleopatra: Rome and Egypt, 69-30 BC

• Britannia: from conquest to province, AD 43-c.84.

How you study

You will look at original ancient sources. There may be the opportunity to visit places such as the Roman Baths at Bath or the British Museum.

How you are assessed

Assessment is by written exam. The questions are a combination of essays and short questions.

What you gain from it

When you study ancient history, you learn to understand and evaluate written material, to express yourself fluently in written and oral communication and to research, organise and present arguments.

After your GCSEs

Further study

You could progress to A level ancient history where you study all aspects of the ancient Greek and Roman world in more depth. You might also progress to history A level where you study British history and different periods of world history.

Ancient history GCSE is useful for other Level 3 qualifications such as BTECs, Cambridge Technicals and T levels as it gives you excellent communication, research and writing skills.

Apprenticeships and training

Ancient history GCSE will be useful for getting into apprenticeships. There are a lot to choose from but you could look at apprenticeships in business and administration, retail, library services, museums, travel and tourism and information technology.

Careers

The study of ancient history shows that you have communication and writing skills as well as research skills and an appreciation of the past and other cultures. This can be useful in many jobs. Examples of directly-relevant jobs would be journalism, publishing, library and museum work, and travel and tourism.

Useful websites

www.warwick.ac.uk/fac/arts/classics/research/outreach/
warwickclassicsnetwork/stoa/anchist/gcse

www.apprenticeships.gov.uk

ART AND DESIGN

Art and design GCSE helps you develop your art skills, ideas and creativity. It will help you to increase your visual awareness and learn different techniques in a variety of media. You learn how to appreciate and analyse works of art, craft and design.

What you study

The topics listed give a broad idea of what you will study. You will need to check with your school or college for the options available to you.

You might study a mixture of different art and design specialisms or concentrate on just one.

Art, craft and design – fine art, graphic communication, textiles, 3D design and photography.

Fine art – drawing, painting, sculpture, installation, lens-/light-based media, photography and the moving image, printmaking, mixed media and land art.

Graphic communication – graphics, design for print, advertising and branding, illustration, package design, typography, interactive design (including web, apps and games), multi-media, motion graphics, signage and exhibition graphics.

Textile design – textiles, fashion design and illustration, costume design, constructed textiles, printed and dyed textiles, surface pattern, stitched and/or embellished textiles, soft furnishings and/or textiles for interiors, digital textiles and installed textiles.

Three-dimensional design – includes architectural design, sculpture, ceramics, product design, jewellery and body adornment, interior design, landscape/garden design, exhibition design, three-dimensional digital design and design for theatre, film and television.

Photography – includes portraiture, location photography, studio photography, experimental imagery, installation, documentary photography, photo-journalism, moving image (film, video and animation), fashion photography.

How you study

You learn different skills and techniques as you work through the course. You will be given projects and design briefs to help build your portfolio of work. You might visit art galleries and exhibitions.

How you are assessed

The course is assessed through a portfolio of work that you prepare throughout the course. There is also a supervised assessment.

What you gain from it

Apart from improving your design, creative and technical skills, you develop your creativity and imagination. You also learn critical and analytical skills and how to make independent decisions. The GCSE can give you confidence and focus.

Even if you don't continue your art and design studies, art and design GCSE is useful to have. Having an insight into art and design can help in your everyday life, for example if you are decorating your house, making your own clothes or taking photographs.

After your GCSEs

Further study

You could continue with art and design A level to develop your skills further. An alternative would be a BTEC National in art and design.

Apprenticeships and training

There are some Level 3 art and design-related apprenticeships available in areas such as floristry, jewellery, bookbinding, tailoring, fashion and in museums and galleries.

Higher/Degree Apprenticeships are available in conservation and in broadcast and media.

You may need additional qualifications (such as A levels or a BTEC Level 3) to enter Higher or Degree Apprenticeships or you may be able to work up through the apprenticeship route.

Careers

You are likely to have to undertake further training in art and design for a design career, depending on your specialism. Even many junior jobs ask for a design degree or apprenticeship.

Once you are trained, there are design jobs in many areas; job titles include games designer, graphic designer, web designer, fashion designer, interior designer, garden designer and product designer. You might also become a professional photographer or animator in the film business.

Related jobs are in retail, such as selling clothes or furniture, or working in an art gallery or museum. Also jobs such as dental technician require artistic skills which you might not expect!

Useful websites

www.bbc.co.uk/bitesize

www.apprenticeships.gov.uk

www.ccskills.org.uk/careers

www.screenskills.com

ASTRONOMY

Are you interested in the night sky and the exploration of the Solar System and Universe? Astronomy GCSE helps you to understand our position in the Universe, the movements of planets and stars, the cycles in the night and daytime sky, and how we use technology to observe and interact with space. You study the science of astronomy and carry out your own observations.

What you study

The topics listed give a broad idea of what you will study. You will need to check with your school or college for the options available to you.

Naked-eye astronomy

- **Planet Earth** – our planet and how it works, its structure and atmosphere.
- **The lunar disc** – the structure surface of the moon, its rotation and revolution.
- **The Earth–Moon–Sun system** – relationship between the Earth, Moon and Sun and how they affect each other, tides, precession and eclipses.
- **Time and the Earth–Moon–Sun cycles** – understanding astronomical definitions and measurements of time. Solstices and equinoxes and the need for time zones.
- **Solar System observation** – how to observe the Sun and planets.
- **Celestial observation** – observing different astronomical phenomena. How to plan observations for the best time and location, taking into account weather and light pollution.
- **Early models of the Solar System** – how ancient civilisations observed and modelled the Solar System.
- **Planetary motion and gravity** – understanding the motion of the planets around the Sun and the role of gravity.

Telescopic astronomy

- **Exploring the Moon** – its internal structure and features.
- **Solar astronomy** – the structure of the Sun, its energy production process and the solar wind.
- **Exploring the Solar System** – the main bodies in the Solar System. How

technology has developed to explore the Solar System, construct probes and land humans on the moon.

- **Formation of planetary systems** – how the interaction of gravitational and tidal forces led to the formation of our Solar System.
- **Exploring starlight** – how stars are observed, how we can obtain information about them from observing the light they emit.
- **Stellar evolution** – how and why stars evolve, how stars form and how they end their life.
- **Our place in the Galaxy** – the Milky Way, our place in it and how it fits into the Universe.
- **Cosmology** – redshift and Hubble's law for distant galaxies. Evidence and explanation for the expanding Universe; dark matter and dark energy and the possible fate of the Universe.

Observations

Throughout the GCSE, you develop observational skills. You must undertake at least one unaided and one aided observation. You need to use your knowledge and understanding of observational techniques and procedures in the written assessments. You record everything you do during observations.

How you study

Apart from learning the theory, you design and make observations. You then analyse and evaluate your observations. You will use star chart apps or a printed star chart and learn how to write up, analyse and evaluate data. You go on visits to observatories or planetariums.

How you are assessed

You are assessed by written exams and for one exam you answer questions about your own astronomical observations.

What you gain from it

You learn maths and physics and gain analytical, observational and recording skills. You develop planning and recording skills as well as learning to use specialised technology.

After your GCSEs

Further study

There isn't an astronomy A level but if you were interested in a career in astronomy, you would need to study physics and maths at A level. You would need a degree in astronomy or physics.

Apprenticeships and training

There are no apprenticeships in astronomy but there are some in space engineering and information technology with satellite and aerospace companies. Companies such as Surrey Satellite Technology, RAL Space, QinetiQ and Airbus recruit apprentices. The National Space Academy runs space engineering apprenticeships leading to a Higher Apprenticeship.

There are some Higher/Degree Apprenticeships in space and aerospace engineering.

You may need additional qualifications (such as A levels or a BTEC Level 3) to enter Higher or Degree Apprenticeships or you may be able to work up through the apprenticeship route.

Careers

A knowledge of astronomy is useful for many careers in maths, science and engineering as you learn how maths and physics are used in astronomy.

Useful websites

www.apprenticeships.gov.uk

www.spacecareers.uk/

www.ras.ac.uk/education-and-careers/careers

www.nationalspaceacademy.org

BIOLOGY

Biology is all about the living world, living organisms (plants and animals) and their structure. It includes the study of the environment and how our own bodies work and how we keep healthy. Biology can lead to many interesting and creative careers in areas like healthcare, research and development.

Sciences are compulsory at Key Stage 4 and can be studied at foundation or higher level. You might study slightly different topics according to the level.

Biology can be studied as a separate subject along with GCSEs in physics and chemistry or as a combined science double award with chemistry and physics.

What you study

Whether you are taking physics GCSE or combined science GCSE, the topics listed give a broad idea of what you will study. You will need to check with your school or college for the options available to you.

• Cell biology – how cells are formed and work

• How digestive and respiratory systems work

• How plants work

• Infection, health problems, cancer

• Bioenergetics – photosynthesis and it how it works

• Our metabolism and nervous system

• Inheritance, variation and evolution

• Ecology – how ecosystems work and how they can be sustained.

How you study

Although you have to learn biological theories in your lessons, practical work forms an important part of the course. You will do practicals throughout the course to put the theoretical study into practice. These practical experiments help you to plan your work, collect and analyse data, develop your investigational skills and learn how to write up the results of your experiments.

How you are assessed

The course is assessed by written exams. They contain a mixture of multiple choice, short answer and extended-response questions. The knowledge and skills gained from practicals is assessed within these exams.

What you gain from it

The important biological principles that you learn help you gain an understanding of how humans, animals and plants function and what is needed to maintain delicate ecosystems in the environment. You learn how to plan your work, conduct experiments and analyse data. You gain investigative and analytical skills and develop your communication skills. It is a creative subject as you learn how to find the best solution to problems.

After your GCSEs

Further study

If you wish to study sciences further you usually need one or two science subjects at A level or equivalent. Most jobs in biology will require higher level qualifications which you can gain by full-time study or whilst working. You are likely to need additional sciences at GCSE or A level for some careers. You could also consider BTEC National qualifications in applied human biology, applied science, health and social care, countryside management or horticulture. T levels may be available in agriculture, animal care, healthcare sciences and science.

Apprenticeships and training

Biology GCSE or biology taken within combined science GCSE is useful for apprenticeships at Level 3 in laboratory work, and also for apprenticeships in veterinary or dental nursing, optical assistant work, animal care, dental technician work, paramedic training, food or animal technology. There are also related apprenticeships in community sport and health, and personal training.

Higher/Degree Apprenticeships lead to training as a dietician, environmental health practitioner, food industry professional, optometrist, play specialist, healthcare scientist, nurse or midwife.

You may need additional qualifications (such as A levels or a BTEC Level 3) to enter Higher or Degree Apprenticeships or you may be able to work up through the apprenticeship route.

Careers

Biology is essential for many careers in healthcare and science and directly relevant jobs include bioscientist, conservationist, doctor, geneticist, zoologist, physiotherapist, radiographer and speech therapist. Some of these careers will need additional sciences for entry.

However the analytical, research and communication skills you learn in biology can be applied to many other career areas including business, finance, information technology and law.

Useful websites

www.bbc.co.uk/bitesize

www.apprenticeships.gov.uk

www.rsb.org.uk

www.healthcareers.nhs.uk

BUSINESS

Everyone either works in a business or has contact with businesses. They range from your hairdresser or local shop right through to huge organisations such as the NHS or British Airways.

Business is not just one subject. It covers a wide variety of topics, including marketing, human resources and finance. You learn business concepts and how to apply ideas to business problems. You find out how businesses operate and the different factors that affect them.

What you study

The topics listed give a broad idea of what you will study. You will need to check with your school or college for the options available to you.

- **Business in the real world** – how businesses are set up, operated and owned, business planning
- **Influences on business** – the impact of technology, for example ecommerce; ethical and environmental considerations, the business climate and economics of business, how globalisation affects business
- **Human resources** – different business structures, recruiting, training and motivating employees
- **Finance** – how business raise finance, cash flow, cash forecasts, financial terms and calculations, financial statements and other business data
- **Marketing** – identifying and understanding customers, market research, costs and methods of marketing.

How you study

You develop business, finance, information technology, communication and problem-solving skills by taking part in practical activities including group work and presentations, as well as studying business case studies. There may be visits to businesses and speakers to provide a real-world insight into the world of business. Maths is going to be very useful for studying business.

How you are assessed

There are written exams with multiple choice questions, short answer questions and extended-writing questions based on business problems.

What you gain from it

You find out how businesses operate which is useful even if you don't intend to start your own business. You learn how to plan your work, solve problems and analyse different types of data. You gain investigative and analytical skills and develop your communication skills.

After your GCSEs

Further study

You could progress to business A level where you will study the subject in depth and work on your decision-making and problem-solving skills. You might also consider BTECs in business, information technology or travel and tourism. There may be T levels available in finance, human resources, law, and management and administration.

Apprenticeships and training

Business GCSE will be useful for apprenticeships at Level 3 in business administration, finance, recruitment, marketing, human resources, retail, travel and logistics.

Higher/Degree Apprenticeships lead to training in accountancy, management consultancy, project management, financial services, banking and retail management.

You may need additional qualifications (such as A levels or a BTEC Level 3) to enter Higher or Degree Apprenticeships or you may be able to work up through the apprenticeship route.

Careers

A knowledge of business is useful for many careers including setting up your own business. There are also specialisms in areas like marketing, human resources, information technology and finance.

Useful websites

www.bbc.co.uk/bitesize

www.apprenticeships.gov.uk

www.businesscasestudies.co.uk

www.bbc.co.uk/news/business

CHEMISTRY

Chemistry is all about understanding the world around us. It includes topics such as the environment, climate change, how recycling works and new developments such as biodiesel. It's a subject that's always changing and developing and by learning the basic principles at GCSE, you can get a qualification relevant to the modern world. You can build on this for many interesting careers in science and healthcare.

Sciences are compulsory at Key Stage 4 and can be studied at foundation or higher level. You might study slightly different topics according to the level.

Chemistry can be studied as a separate subject along with GCSEs in biology and physics or as a combined science double award with physics and biology.

What you study

Whether you are taking chemistry GCSE or combined science GCSE, the topics listed give a broad idea of what you will study. You will need to check with your school or college for the options available to you.

You learn the different theories of chemistry and how they relate to the real world. This will include learning about:

• Atomic structure and the periodic table

• Structure, bonding and the properties of matter

• Chemical changes

• Energy changes in chemistry

• The rate and extent of chemical change

• Chemical analysis

• Chemical and allied industries

• Earth and atmospheric science

• Earth's resources.

How you study

Practical work is an important part of studying science and you will do practicals throughout the course to learn about the different techniques used in chemistry. Undertaking practical experiments helps you to develop your planning skills, collect and analyse data, develop your investigational skills and learn how to write up the results of your experiments.

How you are assessed

The course is assessed by written exams. They contain a mixture of multiple choice, short answer and extended-response questions. The knowledge and skills gained from practicals are assessed within these exams.

What you gain from it

You learn the important theories and rules of chemistry including the periodic table which lists all the chemical elements. You start to gain an understanding of how chemicals react together, how experiments are carried out and how to write up results and process information. You also learn how chemistry helps us to understand the world around us and you gain useful investigative skills.

After your GCSEs

Further study

If you wish to study sciences further you usually need one or two science subjects at A level. Most jobs in chemistry will require higher level qualifications which you might gain by full-time study or whilst working. You could also consider BTEC National qualifications in applied science, or health and social care. T levels may be available in healthcare sciences and science.

Apprenticeships and training

Chemistry GCSE or chemistry taken within combined science GCSE will be useful for apprenticeships at Level 3 training as a laboratory or science manufacturing technician. It will also be useful for apprenticeships in veterinary nursing, animal care, agriculture and horticulture, and apprenticeships training for work as a crop technician, pest control technician, dental nurse, dental technician, paramedic or food technician.

Higher/Degree Apprenticeships can lead to training as a chemical science technologist, life sciences technologist or healthcare science technologist. They could lead to related careers such as becoming a dietician, environmental health practitioner, food industry professional, or in manufacturing and engineering.

You may need additional qualifications (such as A levels or a BTEC Level 3) to enter Higher or Degree Apprenticeships or you may be able to work up through the apprenticeship route.

Careers

Chemistry is essential for many careers and directly-relevant career areas include medicine, pharmacy, forensic science, and research and development in drugs, pesticides, fuels and the food industry. However the investigative and communication skills you learn in chemistry can be applied to many other jobs including business, finance and law.

Useful websites

www.bbc.co.uk/bitesize

www.apprenticeships.gov.uk

www.creative-chemistry.org.uk

www.rsc.org

www.healthcareers.nhs.uk

CITIZENSHIP STUDIES

In citizenship studies you find out what it means to be an 'active citizen'. That is someone who takes an interest in and becomes actively involved with their community and country.

You study a variety of current issues so that you can appreciate different perspectives on how we live together and make decisions in our society. You learn about current debates and issues locally, in your county and globally. Topics include life in the UK, politics and our democracy, law and the rights and responsibilities we have as citizens. You will also get the opportunity to take part in active citizenship by getting involved in a campaign or organisation either locally, nationally or internationally.

What you study

The topics listed give a broad idea of what you will study. You will need to check with your school or college for the options available to you.

- **Rights, the law and the legal system** – rights and responsibilities, law and the legal system (England and Wales)

- **Democracy and government** – democracy, elections and voting in the UK, national, local, regional and devolved government, British constitution, the economy, finance and money, the role of the media and free press, citizenship participation in the UK, politics beyond the UK

- **The UK and the wider world** – identities and diversity in UK society, the UK and its relations with the wider world

- **Citizenship action**
  You take part in some real-life practical activities which may involve research and investigation, problem solving, planning or advocating. You might help with a campaign on a local, national or international level, for example Friends of the Earth or Amnesty International. You could choose to focus on local issues such as recycling facilities, when you might meet with local councillors. You might organise something in your school such as a presentation on climate change or World Aids day.

How you study

Apart from formal lessons you will take part in debates, discussions and presentations as well as involvement in practical community activities.

How you are assessed

There are written exams with multiple choice questions, short answer questions and extended-writing questions.

What you gain from it

You develop knowledge and understanding of the role of a citizen in modern society. You learn what it means to be an active citizen. You develop communication and problem-solving skills by taking part in debates, presentations and community projects.

After your GCSEs

Further study

There is no citizenship studies A level but as this GCSE is a mixture of politics, sociology and economics, you might feel that you would like to continue your studies in these subjects.

Apprenticeships and training

Citizenship GCSE will be useful for apprenticeships in many areas as you will have developed writing and research skills and experience of planning and organising events and making presentations. These skills could apply to many apprenticeships, in business, retail or travel and tourism, for example.

Careers

As citizenship studies is such a broad GCSE, it might inspire you to look at a wide range of careers from community, social work and charity work through to police, the law and jobs in local and national government.

Useful websites

www.bbc.com/bitesize

www.apprenticeships.gov.uk

www.youngcitizens.org

CLASSICAL CIVILISATION

Ancient Rome and Greece have had a major influence on European art, architecture, literature, music, philosophy, politics, law and language. The GCSE will enable you to understand how people lived in ancient times, by looking at classical literature, and historical and archaeological information. You don't need to have knowledge of Latin or ancient Greek as everything is studied in translation.

What you study

The topics listed give a broad idea of what you will study. You will need to check with your school or college for the options available to you.

Thematic study (one studied)

• **Myth and religion** – includes study of the roles, symbols and depictions of the Greek and Roman gods, their festivals and temples, mythology and ancient beliefs in the Underworld.

• **Women in the ancient world** – how women lived in the ancient world and their place in society. The famous women in classical myth and legend such as Helen of Troy, Lucretia and Cleopatra.

Literature and culture (one studied)

• **The Homeric world** – focuses on Homer's Odyssey; the characters and plots and analysis of themes such as fate, revenge and justice. Includes study of real life in the Mycenaean age through sites and artefacts.

• **Roman city life** – everyday life in Roman cities, such as Rome, Ostia, Pompeii and Herculaneum. Aspects of Roman society, housing, education, the social system and entertainment. Authors such as Horace and Juvenal, Petronius and Pliny.

• **War and warfare** – different aspects of warfare in the ancient world. You cover both Greek and Roman civilisation, focusing on Athens and Sparta in the 5th century BC and on Rome in the Imperial period. Military systems and tactics and the interplay between war, politics and society. Key battles and how this impacted on the societies involved. The literature studied is a combination of epic and shorter verse.

How you study

You will look at the original literature in translation and also ancient artefacts. There may be the opportunity to visit places such as the Roman Baths at Bath or the British Museum to view classical collections. You might go on a study trip to Italy or Greece.

How you are assessed

Assessment is by written exam. The questions all require the knowledge of the classical literature and cultural/historical material that you have studied, but some questions will be on unseen material. The questions are a combination of essays and shorter questions.

What you gain from it

Classical civilisation GCSE helps you to understand and evaluate written material as well as ancient artefacts. You learn communication skills by learning how to research, organise and present arguments.

After your GCSEs

Further study

You could progress to A level classical civilisation where you study all aspects of the classical Greek and Roman world in more depth.

Classical civilisation GCSE is useful for other Level 3 qualifications such as BTECs and T levels as it gives you excellent communication, research and writing skills.

Apprenticeships and training

Classical civilisation GCSE might not appear relevant for getting into apprenticeships but there are some directly-related apprenticeships: archaeological technician, museum and galleries technician, and library, information and archive services assistant at Level 3. There are also higher-level apprenticeships in archaeology and conservation although you will need additional A levels or equivalent for these. The skills you will have learnt would be useful in many related apprenticeships in business and administration, retail, travel and information technology.

Careers

The study of classical civilisation shows that you have communication and writing skills as well as research skills and an appreciation of the past and other cultures. This can be useful in many jobs. Examples of directly-relevant jobs are journalism, publishing, library and museum work, archaeology and travel and tourism.

Useful websites

www.apprenticeships.gov.uk

www.classicspage.com

COMPUTER SCIENCE

GCSE computer science explores the principles of digital technology and a way of working that's called 'computational thinking', with coding as a core of the course. You need to be able to think logically, solve puzzles and be persistent when things get difficult. It is a creative subject and satisfying to work out a problem, especially when programming. Knowledge of computer science is connected to many other subjects, especially business, science and maths.

What you study

The topics listed give a broad idea of what you will study. You will need to check with your school or college for the options available to you.

The course gives you an understanding of how computer technology works and a 'behind the scenes' look at the workings of computer systems. You learn a programming language in detail and how to use this language to plan, write and test computer programs.

You also study:

- **Algorithms** – how algorithms work and how they are used to solve problems

- **Programming and coding** – different types of data, concepts and structures in programming, different types of programming languages

- **Computer systems** – hardware and software, systems architecture and storage

- **Computer networks** – different types of networks and protocols

- **Cyber security** – security threats such as phishing, pharming and malicious code, methods to detect and prevent attacks

- **Ethical, legal and environmental impacts of digital technology** – data protection, wearable technology and implants, hacking

- **Software development** – planning, designing, writing, testing and evaluating software

- **Programming project** - developing practical coding and programming skills by working on a real life problem. Produce a report documenting how it was done.

How you study

The course is a mixture of both theory and practical program development. You work on tasks which require you to combine all your skills. You might go on visits to companies or to the Science Museum or National Museum of Computing.

How you are assessed

The course is assessed by written exams where you will be required to work through particular scenarios which will test your computational thinking, problem solving, code tracing and applied computing as well as theoretical knowledge of computer science.

The programming project is not a formal part of the assessment but develops your ability to use the knowledge and skills gained through the course to solve a problem. The skills you learn on this project are tested in the written exams.

What you gain from it

Computer science teaches you to think logically and analytically and to solve problems creatively. These skills will be useful in everyday life and are essential for many careers. Computer skills are likely to be a part of any future career even if you do not become a computer scientist.

After your GCSEs

Further study

You could continue your studies with a computer science A level where you will learn a wider range of programming languages and solve more complex problems. There are BTEC Nationals and T levels in computing.

Apprenticeships and training

Computer science GCSE will be useful for apprenticeships and at Level 3 there are technician-level apprenticeships in cyber security, data security, digital device repair, digital support, and IT solutions software development as well as apprenticeships as a network cable installer and junior content producer.

Higher/Degree Apprenticeships are available as a software tester, cyber intrusion analyst, AI data specialist, cyber security professional, data scientist, digital and technology solutions professional and digital user experience professional.

You may need additional qualifications (such as A levels or a BTEC Level 3) to enter Higher or Degree Apprenticeships or you may be able to work up through the apprenticeship route.

Careers

Careers in computer science include applications developer, computer forensics, cyber security specialist, fin tech (financial technology) specialist, games designer, hardware engineer, IT consultant, network engineer, software engineer, software developer and web developer.

Even if you don't intend to work in computer science, having knowledge of programming, coding and information technology can prove useful for many careers such as business and finance, engineering, construction, science and research.

Useful websites

www.bbc.co.uk/bitesize

www.apprenticeships.gov.uk

www.bcs.org

www.tpdegrees.com/careers

DANCE

GCSE dance is designed to develop your skills in performance and choreography as well as giving you the opportunity to learn and appreciate dance theory by observing, discussing and exploring dance styles.

The course covers a range of dance styles including ballet, urban, contemporary and dance from other cultures. You need to want to dance but also study theory. You don't need to be a wonderful dancer to take this course but you must be motivated to learn and develop your skills.

What you study

The topics listed give a broad idea of what you will study. You will need to check with your school or college for the options available to you.

Performance

- Physical skills required for performance such as posture, balance, coordination and control.
- Technical dance skills such as action content (e.g. travel, turn, elevation, gesture) and dynamic content (e.g. fast/slow, sudden/sustained, acceleration/deceleration, flowing/abrupt).
- Movement in different spaces, timing and rhythm. Expressive skills including projection, focus, spatial awareness, facial expression and phrasing. Dancing with other dancers.
- Mental skills including movement memory, commitment, concentration, confidence and discipline. Accepting criticism and feedback.
- Safe working practices such as how to dance safely by warming up and cooling down properly, appropriate nutrition, hydration, clothing and footwear.

Choreography

- How dances are choreographed and the different elements involved like movement and use of space.
- Different processes for choreographing a dance such research, improvisation, development, structure and refining and synthesising.
- The sound used which could be singing, spoken word and orchestra or silence.

26

- Places where you might perform such as a theatre, studio or a non-theatre site, or even in the street.

Dance appreciation

How to evaluate and criticise your own work, the study of set works to develop knowledge of different dance companies, styles and choreographers and critical skills.

Examples of set works:

- Artificial Things – Stopgap Dance Company – choreographer Lucy Bennett
- A Linha Curva – Rambert Dance Company – choreographer Itzik Galili
- Infra – The Royal Ballet – choreographer Wayne McGregor
- Shadows – Phoenix Dance Theatre – choreographer Christopher Bruce
- Within Her Eyes – James Cousins Company – choreographer James Cousins.

You look at all aspects of these works: performance space, dance content, movement, structure and atmosphere of the piece.

How you study

Lessons are a mixture of theory and practical. In theory you might research a particular choreographer and a piece of work, watch a DVD, take part in a class discussion of that work and share your own evaluation.

For practical work you might follow a teacher, work on your own or with a partner, learn dance material in either solo or group form or create your own dance.

You have to be independent and work on your own ideas, as well as being prepared to work in groups. There will be rehearsals that might take place during breaks or after school. There will be the opportunity to attend dance performances.

How you are assessed

60% of the GCSE marks are through an assessment of your practical dance and choreography skills. There is a solo performance and then a solo or group choreography. 40% of the marks are assessed on dance appreciation with a written exam to test your knowledge and understanding of choreographic processes and performing skills, as well as demonstrating critical appreciation of your own and professional works.

What you gain from it

GCSE dance increases your confidence and self-esteem, improves problem solving and creativity and allows you to make knowledgeable decisions about dances. It promotes fitness, a healthy lifestyle, self-discipline, leadership, teamwork and creativity.

After your GCSEs

Further study

You could progress to dance A level or consider related qualifications such as a BTEC in dance or performing arts.

Apprenticeships and training

Dance GCSE is useful for apprenticeships at Level 3 as a costume performance technician, creative venue technician and live event technician. Higher/Degree Apprenticeships are available in creative industries in jobs such as production manager. Dancing apprenticeships are available at postgraduate level.

You may need additional qualifications (such as A levels or a BTEC Level 3) to enter Higher or Degree Apprenticeships or you may be able to work up through the apprenticeship route.

Careers

Apart from becoming a performer or choreographer, there are jobs such as teacher, dance movement therapist, dance project manager, costume/set designer and dance photographer, and opportunities in dance press and public relations, and journalism.

Useful websites

www.apprenticeships.gov.uk

www.cdmt.org.uk (for accredited dance schools)

www.onedanceuk.org

DESIGN AND TECHNOLOGY

Everything has to be designed; this could be desks, chairs, pens and pencils, phones, tablets or the carton for our breakfast cereal. Design and technology is a creative and practical subject. It is about how products are designed and made, the different technologies involved, the different materials that can be used and the problems that must be overcome. It offers the opportunity to learn design skills and to design and make your own products.

What you study

The topics listed give a broad idea of what you will study. You will need to check with your school or college for the options available to you.

- Different technologies for designing products, including developments in new materials, ways of developing and designing products; materials and their properties. You might specialise in one particular material such as metal, paper and board, polymers, textiles or timber.

- Selecting different materials or components taking into account their ecological and social footprint. Sourcing materials and how to work with them. Product production and specialist techniques and processes, surface treatments and finishes.

- How to design and develop prototypes in response to clients' requirements. How to design a new and innovative product whilst making it marketable. Evaluating prototypes, suggesting modifications and improvements and improved manufacturing processes, assessing if prototypes are fit for purpose. The prototype product could be an everyday item like a clock or lamp but could be a piece of equipment for someone with disabilities; there are endless possibilities.

How you study

The GCSE is a mixture of theory and practical work. You learn theory and put it into practice by doing small projects, as well as your main design and make project. You might have to put in extra time in the workshop when you are working on your main project.

How you are assessed

The written exam is a mixture of multiple choice and short and extended questions assessing your technical knowledge and understanding.

Design and make task

You produce a prototype and a portfolio of evidence demonstrating your practical understanding and application of the design and technical principles that you have learned on the course. It accounts for 50% of the marks.

As part of the GCSE, your maths and science skills will also be assessed.

What you gain from it

You learn how a product is designed from start to finish so the GCSE gives you an insight into the business side of manufacturing as well as the practical side. You learn how to plan your work, solve problems and work to a design brief. You gain investigative and analytical skills and develop your communication skills.

After your GCSEs

Further study

You could progress to design and technology A level where you could specialise in design engineering, fashion and textiles or product design. If you are considering progressing in design and technology you may need maths and science A levels. You might also consider related qualifications such as a BTEC or T levels.

Apprenticeships and training

There is a wide range of apprenticeships where you might use your design and technology GCSE as it is such a versatile subject. Examples at Level 3 in engineering are accident repair technician, bicycle mechanic, bus and coach technician, engineering design or engineering technician. You could consider an apprenticeship as a boat builder, fashion and textile technician, footwear manufacturer, furniture technician, garment maker or dental technician.

Higher/Degree Apprenticeships related to design and technology are available in engineering, manufacture and construction.

You may need additional qualifications (such as A levels or a BTEC Level 3) to enter Higher or Degree Apprenticeships or you may be able to work up through the apprenticeship route.

Careers

The skills you learn in design and technology are useful in careers in engineering, product design and manufacture. You will have knowledge of different materials, the production process and will have developed technical and practical skills. You also have knowledge of business so even if you don't want to use your skills to become a product designer, you will have gained useful business and communication skills.

Useful websites

www.bbc.co.uk/bitesize

www.apprenticeships.gov.uk

www.institution-engineering-designers.org.uk

DRAMA

In GCSE drama you gain an understanding of drama through studying different plays and devising your own. You evaluate plays and analyse how they are put together. You apply this knowledge to your performances as you develop your practical skills. You can be a performer but also experience different roles such as design, lighting, sound, set or costume.

What you study

The topics listed give a broad idea of what you will study. You will need to check with your school or college for the options available to you.

Theory

You study plays and learn the theory, history and other aspects of drama. There will be set plays and you experience live performances of plays and look at how they are put together and all aspects of the production.

Performance

You create your own performance (known as devised drama) working in a group. You will be able to take on different tasks within the group such as costumes or directing. You may write a log or blog describing how you went about this and the different techniques you used.

You perform extracts from set plays which could be anything from Shakespeare right through to more modern plays such as Blood Brothers by Willy Russell.

How you study

Lessons are a mixture of theory and practical, so you must enjoy both. For practical work you will be working in a group, rehearsing and improvising or be involved in other aspects of a production such as lighting or stage management.

You have to be prepared to work on your own ideas, as well as being able to work in a group.

There will be rehearsals that might take place during breaks or after school. There may be the opportunity to attend live theatre performances.

How you are assessed

40% of the drama GCSE marks are assessed through a written exam with multiple choice and longer answers on what you have studied. 60% of the marks are from the assessment of your practical work; you are assessed on the performances you have created as well as your individual performance or other work e.g. directing or costumes.

What you gain from it

You develop the skills involved in creating and performing drama and also communication, presentation/public speaking, group and leadership skills, problem solving, time management, initiative and the ability to work to a deadline. The study of drama helps you become more self-confident and prepares you to deal with a range of different situations and people. These skills will be useful to you even if you don't intend to have a career in drama.

After your GCSEs

Further study

You could progress to drama A level or consider related qualifications such as a BTEC in performing arts.

Apprenticeships

Drama GCSE will be useful for apprenticeships at Level 3 as an assistant puppet maker, costume performance technician, creative venue technician, live event technician and props technician.

Higher/Degree Apprenticeships are available in areas such as drama therapy and creative industries production management.

You may need additional qualifications (such as A levels or a BTEC Level 3) to enter Higher or Degree Apprenticeships or you may be able to work up through the apprenticeship route.

Careers

You don't need a drama diploma or degree to become an actor, or to work elsewhere in the theatre, but taking such a qualification can help as it will give you further performance training and experience, and contacts to help you find work. Don't forget that there are lots of other jobs connected with drama such props technician, technical theatre work, costumes, directing and there is also the business side, which includes production, theatre management and box office, or jobs in accountancy or marketing for theatres.

However, the confidence that you gain through drama will be useful in whatever career you choose. You will have no trouble speaking and giving presentations to a group for example and that could apply to many jobs and careers.

Useful websites

www.bbc.co.uk/bitesize

www.apprenticeships.gov.uk

www.ccskills.org.uk/careers/advice/any/theatre

www.getintotheatre.org

www.federationofdramaschools.co.uk

www.nyt.org.uk

ECONOMICS

Economics is all about the world around you and how it operates. GCSE economics gives you the chance to investigate and evaluate what affects, for example, the price of consumer goods, employment opportunities and the impact of globalisation. It's is a real-world subject, with events continually happening which affect markets and the economy, not only in the UK but globally.

What you study

The topics listed give a broad idea of what you will study. You will need to check with your school or college for the options available to you.

- **How markets work** – production, costs, revenue and profit, resource allocation, how prices are determined. Different types of markets and how they fail.

- **How the economy works** – How the national economy functions, what objectives a government may want to achieve, and the policy options which they have to meet these objectives. How our increasingly globalised economy operates and how this can affect other countries. The role of money and financial markets.

When studying these topics you learn to perform calculations such as percentages, averages, costs and profit. You also learn to construct graphs from data and how to interpret and analyse the information to support economic decisions.

How you study

There will be theory classes, group discussions and presentations. You learn techniques for working with numerical, graphical and written data to analyse economic issues. You carry out research and share your thoughts and opinions on the economic climate.

You need to read widely about economics and read a quality 'broadsheet' newspaper such as the Guardian, The Times, The Independent or the Financial Times. You might go on a visit to an employer or financial institution.

How you are assessed

You are assessed through written exams which include multiple choice questions and some extended-writing questions based on economic problems and case studies. Some answers will require undertaking calculations.

What you gain from it

You learn how the economy operates which is useful whatever you plan to do. The subject also teaches you to be a creative and critical thinker and how to make justified decisions.

You learn how to plan your work, carry out research, solve problems and analyse different types of data. You gain investigative and analytical skills. You learn to work with others and gain communication skills by taking part in discussions and debates.

After your GCSEs

Further study

You could progress to economics A level where you will study the subject in depth. You might also consider related qualifications such as a BTEC National in business or a T level in finance.

Apprenticeships and training

Economics GCSE will be useful for apprenticeships at Level 3 in accountancy, business, finance, retail and taxation.

Higher/Degree Apprenticeships lead to training in accountancy, management consultancy, project management, financial services, banking and retail management. There is a Degree Apprenticeship to train as a professional economist.

You may need additional qualifications (such as A levels or a BTEC Level 3) to enter Higher or Degree Apprenticeships or you may be able to work up through the apprenticeship route.

Careers

An economics GCSE could be useful for working in many businesses or organisations. It would be especially useful in careers in business, finance and retail. There are professional economists who work for the government, in the financial sector and for lots of other organisations.

Useful websites

www.apprenticeships.gov.uk

http://whystudyeconomics.ac.uk

www.gov.uk/government/organisations/civil-service-government-economic-service

ENGINEERING

In GCSE engineering you learn engineering theory and the skills needed to help you solve engineering problems. You learn how to create design briefs, how businesses convert design briefs to design specifications, production planning and the application of technology to manufacturing.

What you study

The topics listed give a broad idea of what you will study. You will need to check with your school or college for the options available to you.

Engineering materials – different types of engineering materials such as metals, polymers and composites, their different properties and uses. Material costs and supply, and factors that influence how you solve design problems such as environmentally-friendly methods of production.

Engineering manufacturing processes – how different manufacturing processes work in constructing, shaping and finishing products.

Systems – different systems for manufacturing products e.g. electrical, electronic or pneumatic.

Testing and investigation – different methods of testing products to make sure they meet the brief.

The impact of modern technologies – how new technologies might affect the environment, society or economics of a country.

Practical engineering skills – the important engineering skills you need, for example producing engineering drawings, using computer-aided engineering (CAD) and selecting the right tools and methods for the job.

For the practical assessment you engineer a product to a given brief. Your maths skills will be important in this GCSE.

How you study

It's a mixture of theory and practical work. You carry out some independent research, participate in group work and role play, use real business resources and benefit from the advice of people who are actually working in engineering when you visit engineering companies or have speakers.

How you are assessed

The written exam is multiple choice, short and longer answers including calculations. This will assess how you apply your practical engineering skills.

Practical engineering is examined through an extended project brief where you design, prototype and manufacture your own design to a set brief from the exam board. You produce a portfolio explaining how you went about the project.

What you gain from it

The theory and practical work involved teach you useful skills that you may use even if you don't go into engineering. You learn to think logically in order to write engineering plans and learn to work and research on your own and as part of a group. It is a creative subject as you work out the best solution to problems.

After your GCSEs

Further study

You could progress to A levels in design and technology: design engineering or design and technology: product design. If you are considering a career in engineering it would be a good idea to consider A levels in physics and maths.

You might also consider related qualifications such as BTECs in engineering or specialist types of engineering, e.g. aeronautical engineering, electrical/ electronic engineering, manufacturing engineering or mechanical engineering. There are T levels in manufacturing, construction and building services engineering.

Apprenticeships and training

Engineering GCSE will be useful for apprenticeships as an engineering technician where you could be working in a range of sectors such as marine, transport, building services, civil engineering, construction, refrigeration, gas and other utilities. You could specialise in digital engineering or design engineering. There are many different types of engineering apprenticeships available and for these you will need good grades in GCSE maths and English.

Some apprenticeships allow progression to Higher/Degree Apprenticeships in career areas such as manufacturing, aerospace, electronic engineering, materials science, the nuclear industry, mechanical and electrical engineering, power engineering, space and rail engineering.

You may need additional qualifications (such as A levels or a BTEC Level 3) to enter Higher or Degree Apprenticeships or you may be able to work up through the apprenticeship route.

Careers

GCSE engineering can lead to many careers and directly-related jobs as well as engineering of all types. It will be useful in design engineering or product/industrial design. Your skills in research, logical thinking and knowledge of product manufacture will be useful in many business careers and your knowledge of information technology could lead to careers in computing.

Useful websites

www.apprenticeships.gov.uk

www.tomorrowsengineers.org.uk

ENGLISH LANGUAGE

GCSE English language is vital in today's job market and a minimum requirement for many courses. It is designed to develop your confidence and skills in speaking and listening, reading and writing. It will help improve your grammar, spelling and punctuation, vocabulary, encourage active reading and develop your ability to write for different audiences and purposes.

English language is one of the compulsory subjects at Key Stage 4.

What you study

The topics listed give a broad idea of what you will study. You will need to check with your school or college for the options available to you.

Reading

You read a range of texts from different periods of literature from the 19th, 20th and 21st centuries. You look at a wide range of literature, both fiction and nonfiction, and also examples of other writing such as journalism, diaries, essays and travel writing.

You examine how the writers use narrative and descriptive techniques to capture the interest of readers. You need to be able to comprehend what you have read and to analyse the text and look at it critically. You look at the author's viewpoint and see how they were influenced by the period they were writing in and how this affected their perspective.

Writing and speaking

You learn to write effectively and clearly for different audiences and for different purposes. This means using the right vocabulary, punctuation and grammar as well as being creative and imaginative. You learn how to make the right impact and impression with your work by emphasising facts, ideas and key points, using evidence to support your views or to make an emotional impact. You need to be able to judge the context, so you use appropriate vocabulary and tone when writing or speaking.

How you study

You study texts in class and learn grammar and vocabulary. There are written and spoken assignments and comprehension exercises.

How you are assessed

Assessment is by written exam answering short, longer and extended questions. There is a spoken English assessment where you might give a presentation or take part in a debate or interview. The spoken English assessment is not part of your main GCSE grade but appears as an additional mark on your GCSE result.

What you gain from it

Having a good command of written and spoken English will give you confidence. You will be able to communicate your ideas better and it will develop your critical and analytical skills. Having an English language GCSE is an essential requirement for many careers, even if you plan to study a practical or scientific course. Good communication skills are highly valued by employers.

After your GCSEs

Further study

You could progress to A level English language where you study the language in more depth and learn to write for specific audiences and purposes. You might also want to consider A level English literature and other A levels where you might use your language skills such as history or sociology.

English language GCSE is useful for other Level 3 qualifications such as BTECs and T levels as you will be able to use the communication skills, both written and spoken, that you have gained from the GCSE.

Apprenticeships and training

English language GCSE will be useful for any apprenticeship and is sometimes essential. There are a lot to choose from but you could look at apprenticeships in business and administration, retail, library services and digital and information technology. There are T levels in management and administration, and in human resources.

Careers

English language skills are essential whatever career you choose as you need to be able to communicate effectively to be successful. Examples of relevant career areas are journalism, film and media, publishing, library work, marketing and advertising.

Useful websites

www.bbc.co.uk/bitesize

www.apprenticeships.gov.uk

www.nctj.com

www.bookcareers.com

www.screenskills.com

www.intofilm.org

ENGLISH LITERATURE

Do you like reading and thinking about what you have read and how it has been written? English literature GCSE involves reading a wide range of novels, plays and poetry. You learn to read critically, understand, enjoy and respond to all types of different books, poetry and plays. The literature studied ranges from Shakespeare right up to the present day.

Through studying English literature you analyse how the authors created their works and it also gives you an awareness of the history, culture and social attitudes of the period in which the works were written. The GCSE will improve your writing skills and use of English.

English is one of the compulsory subjects at Key Stage 4. Some schools might just ask you to take English language but most will require English literature.

What you study

The topics listed give a broad idea of what you will study. You will need to check with your school or college for the options available to you.

- **Shakespeare** – examples are *Romeo and Juliet, The Merchant of Venice, Macbeth* or *Much Ado About Nothing*

- **19th century novel** – examples are *Great Expectations* by Charles Dickens, *Jane Eyre by* Charlotte Brontë, *Pride and Prejudice* by Jane Austen

- **Poetry** – you study a selection of poetry; examples of poets you might study include John Keats, Emily Brontë, Gerard Manly Hopkins, Philip Larkin, Liz Lochhead and Carol Anne Duffy

- **British fiction or drama** – from 1919 to the present day; examples are *Anita and Me* by Meera Syal, *Never Let Me Go* by Kazuo Ishiguro, *Animal Farm* by George Orwell, *An Inspector Calls* by J. B. Priestley, *DNA* by Dennis Kelly.

How you study

You study each work as a whole but may also write about an extract from it. You also look at unseen texts and learn to analyse and criticise them. You may have the opportunity to see some plays as part of the course.

How you are assessed

Assessment is by written exam on your set texts. Some specifications include an unseen text that you will analyse.

What you gain from it

GCSE English literature gives you confidence in communicating ideas and will improve your writing skills. It develops your critical and analytical skills. It also gives you an insight into the history and culture of the periods studied.

After your GCSEs

Further study

You could progress to A level English literature where you study a wider variety of literature in more depth and do a lot more independent reading and research around the texts. English literature GCSE is useful for other Level 3 qualifications such as BTECs and T levels as you will be able to use the communication skills that you have gained from the GCSE.

Apprenticeships and training

English literature GCSE will be useful for entry into apprenticeships. There are a lot to choose from but you could look at apprenticeships in business and administration, retail, library services and digital and information technology.

Careers

The study of English literature shows that you have communication and writing skills as well as the ability to look critically and analyse the written word and this can be useful in many jobs. Examples of directly-related jobs would be journalism, publishing, library work, media and film, marketing and advertising.

Useful websites

www.bbc.co.uk/bitesize

www.apprenticeships.gov.uk

www.nctj.com

www.bookcareers.com

www.screenskills.com

www.intofilm.org

FILM STUDIES

Film is a major art form and an important and expanding industry, especially as there are now many ways to watch films apart from the cinema. GCSE film studies teaches you about how films are made in Britain, Hollywood and all over the world. You study a variety of films and the ways in which they are experienced in today's global society. You investigate the place film has in communicating ideas, attitudes and cultural beliefs, both now and in the past.

What you study

The topics listed give a broad idea of what you will study. You will need to check with your school or college for the options available to you.

You study six films and in each one you look at:

- The key elements of film form and how they fit together (cinematography, mise-en-scène, editing and sound)
- The contexts of film (social, cultural, historical, political and institutional), including key aspects of the history of film and film technology.

Examples of the films are:

1. US Films – mainstream and independent films from different eras

- Examples of mainstream films are: King Solomon's Mines, Raiders of the Lost Ark, Singin' in the Rain, Grease, Rear Window, Rebel without a Cause and E.T. the Extra-Terrestrial.
- Examples of independently produced US films are: Little Miss Sunshine, The Hurt Locker, and Me and Earl and the Dying Girl.

2. Global Films – global films, produced outside the US. Includes UK films (made since 2010), English language films and films in other languages

- Examples are: Rabbit-Proof Fence, Slumdog Millionaire and Song of the Sea.
- Examples of non-English language films are: Spirited Away, Let the Right One In and Wadjda.
- UK films (produced since 2010) include Submarine, Attack the Block and Skyfall.

Production task – you write a screenplay or make your own short film. You write an analysis of your work and evaluate it to see how it compares with professional films or screenplays.

How you study

You watch the set films, looking at their structure, how they were filmed and the different elements used to put them together. You look at the background and history of the film as well as the content and how it gets its point over. There will be discussions and debates about each film.

You learn the practical side of film making, carrying out research and working in groups to complete your project. They may be visits to film studios and screenings.

How you are assessed

Assessment is by written exams answering short, longer and extended questions plus the production task.

What you gain from it

Apart from gaining an insight into the film industry and the different skills involved, you gain confidence in your critical and analytical skills. You learn communication skills through your written work as well as visual communication skills. You acquire teamwork skills through working as a team with other students.

After your GCSEs

Further study

You could progress to A level film studies or media studies or to a Level 3 qualification such as a BTEC in creative digital media production . There is a T level in media, broadcast and production.

Apprenticeships and training

Film studies GCSE will be useful for Level 3 apprenticeships in broadcast and media as, for example, a systems technical operator, digital marketer, broadcast production assistant or junior content designer. There are Level 4 apprenticeships in visual effects. Organisations offering apprenticeships include ITV and the BBC.

Higher/Degree Apprenticeships are available as a broadcast and media systems technician or broadcast and media systems engineer.

You may need additional qualifications (such as A levels or a BTEC Level 3) to enter Higher or Degree Apprenticeships or you may be able to work up through the apprenticeship route.

Careers

There are career opportunities in film as it is an expanding industry. You may need to get further qualifications to gain more experience and useful industry contacts. Some people start as a runner or assistant as a first step in the industry. There are also jobs such as camera operator, screen/script writer director and producer and opportunities in visual effects (VFX).

Useful websites

www.bbc.co.uk/bitesize

www.apprenticeships.gov.uk

www.screenskills.com

www.intofilm.org

FOOD PREPARATION AND NUTRITION

GCSE food preparation and nutrition equips you with the knowledge, understanding and skills required to cook and teaches you about food science, nutrition and healthy eating. You learn to make informed decisions about food and nutrition and gain the knowledge to be able to feed yourself and others affordably and nutritiously, now and later in life. Even if you don't intend to enter the catering or hospitality industry, the skills you learn will be really valuable to you and the course gives you the chance to be creative.

What you study

The topics listed give a broad idea of what you will study. You will need to check with your school or college for the options available to you.

- **Food, nutrition and health** – the relationship between diet and health, nutritional and dietary needs of different groups of people and how to take these into account when selecting recipes. Protein, fat, carbohydrates, vitamins, minerals, water, the nutritional content of food.

- **Food science** – how food is cooked, different cooking methods, chemical properties of food.

- **Food safety** – food spoilage and contamination, buying and storing food, safely preparing, cooking and serving food.

- **Food choice** – factors that influence food choice, such as food allergies, food labelling, British and international cuisines.

- **Food provenance** – environmental impact and the sustainability of food. How are ingredients grown, reared or caught; different types of farming such as organic, intensive and sustainable. Food processing methods.

- **Cooking and food preparation skills** – knife skills, preparation of fruits and vegetables, marinating, shaping, making sauces, baking, bread making and a range of cooking processes.

How you study

There will be some theory lessons. Written work will involve planning your work and recipes and you will cook regularly.

How you are assessed

There are written exams, a written food investigation project in some specifications and also a food preparation assessment where you will prepare, cook and present a meal within a certain time. This will assess knowledge of planning, preparation, cooking and presentation skills.

What you gain from it

You gain invaluable cooking skills and a good knowledge of nutrition and healthy eating. The written work gives you skills in planning your work as well as investigative and analytical skills.

After your GCSEs

Further study

You could progress to a Level 3 qualification in food science and nutrition (WJEC) where you will study the subject in depth and learn further skills. You could also consider the BTEC in hospitality and catering or a professional chef diploma. There is a T level in catering.

Apprenticeships and training

This GCSE will be useful for apprenticeships at Level 3 to become a professional chef, baker or hospitality supervisor.

Higher/Degree Apprenticeships lead to training in hospitality management or food science and technology.

You may need additional qualifications (such as A levels or a BTEC Level 3) to enter Higher or Degree Apprenticeships or you may be able to work up through the apprenticeship route.

Careers

There are many possible careers in this growing area including chef, waiter, restaurant manager, housekeeper, food scientist, dietician, nutritionist and jobs in food production. Food science and technology is shortage area.

Useful websites

www.bbc.co.uk/bitesize (see Home Economics)

www.apprenticeships.gov.uk

www.tastesuccess.co.uk

www.tastycareers.org.uk

GEOGRAPHY

Geography is an important subject in today's world and matters related to geography are always in the news. So many of the world's problems are connected to geography; for example global warming, sustainable food production, natural disasters such as earthquakes and tsunamis, the spread of disease, the reasons for migration and future energy sources. A knowledge and understanding of geography will be in great demand to help solve these challenges.

What you study

The topics listed give a broad idea of what you will study. You will need to check with your school or college for the options available to you.

Geography is made up of human and physical geography:

- Physical geography is all about the earth and its structure and how it works.

- Human geography is about the activities of humans and how they interact with the earth.

Physical geography

- How ecosystems work such as tropical rain forests and deserts

- Different types of landscapes in the UK and how they work; river, coastal and glacial landscapes

- Natural hazards such as earthquakes and hurricanes

- Climate change; how it is caused by both manmade and natural hazards.

Human geography

- Population and migration in the UK and globally

- How cities have grown; economic and social factors of living in cities, urban regeneration

- Housing and transport, the environment, sustainability; food water and energy.

Practical applications and fieldwork

You learn how to tackle and solve geographical problems and present arguments in a logical way using different types of evidence. Fieldwork is an important part of the course and you will undertake fieldwork and write up your findings.

Geographical skills

You learn the essential skills used by geographers:

• Maps: how they are constructed, how to interpret them and mapmaking skills including using GIS (Geographical Information Systems)

• Using different types of data and statistics to represent different types of information

• Writing skills to produce reports and surveys and to communicate different types of information to different audiences.

How you study

Apart from formal lessons, there will be debates and discussions and you learn to use GIS systems such as Google Earth and other software tools. You also learn how to write up reports correctly and accurately using different data sources. Fieldwork is an important part of the course. It might consist of a day trip or a residential, for example in Snowdonia or the Lake District.

How you are assessed

There are written exams with multiple choice questions, short answer questions and extended-writing questions based on geographical issues.

What you gain from it

You gain knowledge of the physical world around you, how it works as well as how humans impact on it. You also learn critical thinking and problem-solving skills. You learn how to plan your work, solve problems and analyse different types of data. You gain investigative and analytical skills and develop your communication skills.

After your GCSEs

Further study

You could progress to geography or environmental science A level where you will study the subject in more depth. You might also consider related qualifications such a BTEC in countryside management, forestry and arboriculture, applied science or travel and tourism. There is a T level in science.

Apprenticeships and training

Geography GCSE will be useful for apprenticeships at Level 3 as a water environment worker, and as a safety, health and environment technician.

Higher/Degree apprenticeships lead to training as an environmental practitioner, ecologist or town planner.

You may need additional qualifications (such as A levels or a BTEC Level 3) to enter Higher or Degree apprenticeships or you may be able to work up through the apprenticeship route.

Careers

A knowledge of geography is useful for many careers such as town planning, cartography (mapmaking), environmental and conservation work, landscape architecture, business or economic development or work in local and national government. You can now study disaster management at degree level. You may need further study to qualify in some of these careers.

Useful websites

www.bbc.co.uk/bitesize

www.apprenticeships.gov.uk

www.rgs.org

www.ordnancesurvey.co.uk/careers

GEOLOGY

Geology is all about the structure of the Earth: how it was formed, the materials it's made of and the processes acting upon it. You learn how the Earth works and about its mineral and energy resources. Geology is also known as Earth science or geoscience. You find out how an understanding and application of Earth science is vital to the future of the world, from supplying the demand for mineral, energy and water resources to finding out how natural hazards can have less impact through improved engineering and prediction techniques.

What you study

The topics listed give a broad idea of what you will study. You will need to check with your school or college for the options available to you.

- **Geological principles** – minerals, the three major rock types (igneous, sedimentary and metamorphic) and how they were formed, the rock cycle, plate tectonics, global climate and sea level change, fossils, concepts in geological time, planetary geology (i.e. the Moon, other planets, comets and asteroids), geohazards such as volcanoes, earthquakes, landslides and tsunamis, natural resources, and how human interaction with the Earth can increase or reduce risk of Earth hazards.

- **Investigative skills and techniques** – identifying and testing samples of rocks or fossils. Using geological maps and diagrams. Learning to handle and analyse data.

- **Fieldwork** – an important part of the course and you carry out two days of fieldwork. You will learn to identify a range of minerals, rocks and fossils and this practical work helps develop field observation and practical skills.

How you study

There will be formal lessons and practical activities in the classroom as well as practical fieldwork. There will be trips to places of geological interest that could be in your local area or to places further afield such as the Lake District or the Jurassic coast.

How you are assessed

There are two written papers:

Geological principles – multiple choice, short, structured and extended-writing answers. This is an onscreen exam with data given to you.

Investigative geology – short, structured and extended-writing answers to investigate the geology of an area shown on a simplified geological map.

The assessment places strong emphasis on the practical skills you will have learnt in geology. This includes the use of mathematics, the interpretation of geological maps and geological histories, and the identification and description of minerals, rocks and fossils .

What you gain from it

You gain an understanding of how the Earth came into being and how it works. You develop skills and techniques in the analysis and interpretation of data, problem solving and writing up and presenting data.

After your GCSEs

Further study

GCSE geology can lead to A level geology, and overlaps with topics studied in both A level geography and environmental science. You might also consider related qualifications such a BTEC in environmental sustainability, applied science or engineering. There is a T level in science.

Apprenticeships and training

Geology GCSE will be useful for apprenticeships at Level 3 working as a laboratory technician which could lead to training as a geotechnician.

Higher/Degree apprenticeships lead to training as an environmental practitioner or ecologist.

You may need additional qualifications (such as A levels or a BTEC Level 3) to enter Higher or Degree apprenticeships or you may be able to work up through the apprenticeship route.

Careers

A knowledge of geology is essential for many careers such as pollution control, surveying, water supply, engineering geology, renewable energy and geotechnical engineering. It can also be useful for careers in town planning, cartography (mapmaking) and environmental and conservation work. You may need to undertake further study to for entry to some of these careers. Jobs for qualified geologist/geoscientists are projected to grow in the future as the need for energy and environmental protection grows.

Useful websites

www.bbc.co.uk/bitesize

www.apprenticeships.gov.uk

www.geolsoc.org.uk

GREEK (CLASSICAL)/LATIN

These two GCSEs give you the opportunity to learn the ancient Greek and Latin languages (ancient Greek is known as classical Greek) and to learn about the culture of ancient Greece and Rome, You will also study some of the literature from both these civilisations. The cultures of ancient Greece and Rome are fascinating to study in themselves but they are also the foundation of modern Western civilisation and cultures.

By studying classical Greek or Latin, you begin to appreciate the language and literature, history and society of the classical world and begin to understand how it has influenced our own.

What you study

The topics listed give a broad idea of what you will study. You will need to check with your school or college for the options available to you.

- **Language** – you learn the basics of the language which includes the grammar and vocabulary. You will study texts and stories. You learn to translate passages from the original ancient Greek /Latin. You discover how some English words come from ancient Greek /Latin.

- **Classical texts** – you will study classical set texts and answer questions on them (in English).

  - For classical Greek these might include works by Herodotus, Homer, Plutarch, Lucian and Plato.

  - For Latin these might include works by Virgil, Pliny, Tacitus, Ovid, Martial, Horace and Cicero.

- **Civilisation and culture** – you study the history and culture of ancient Greece/ Rome and cover topics such as their religion, myths and beliefs, entertainment and for Latin you might study the Romans in Britain.

How you study

You read the original literature in translation and study ancient artefacts. There may be the opportunity to visit places such as the Roman Baths at Bath or the British Museum to view classical collections. You might go on a study tour to Italy or Greece.

How you are assessed

You are tested on your language knowledge by doing translations and/or answering comprehension questions about unseen texts. You answer comprehension questions and/or translate parts of your set texts and answer questions about your culture and history studies.

What you gain from it

Studying an ancient language helps you understand the way languages are structured, and how they impact upon later cultures. It also equips you with logical and analytical skills and will help you if you want to study modern foreign languages, English, history or classics. Latin is also very useful if you intend to study law.

After your GCSEs

Further study

You could progress to A level in Greek (classical) or Latin where you study the language, history and culture in more depth.

Apprenticeships and training

A GCSE in either classical Greek or Latin might not appear relevant for getting into apprenticeships but it could be useful for apprenticeships in museums or libraries. There are apprenticeships as a museum and galleries technician and library, information and archive services assistant at Level 3. There are also higher-level apprenticeships in archaeology and conservation.

The skills you will have learnt would be useful in many related apprenticeships in business and administration, retail, travel and information technology.

Careers

The study of ancient Greek or Latin shows that you have communication and writing skills as well as research skills and an appreciation of the past and other cultures. It also shows that you have language skills which will be helpful if you need to learn modern languages. This can be useful in many jobs. Examples of career areas are journalism, publishing, library and museum work, archaeology and travel and tourism.

Useful websites

www.apprenticeships.gov.uk

www.classicspage.com

HISTORY

History is all about when and why events happened and what we can learn from them. In GCSE history you study key events in history and get to understand how they shaped modern society. You study historical periods from medieval times up to the present day including British, European and worldwide history.

What you study

The topics listed give a broad idea of what you will study. You will need to check with your school or college for the options available to you.

You study different topics over different time periods, by thematic study or a study in depth. Examples are:

Period study

• Viking expansion, c.750– c.1050

• The Mughal Empire, 1526–1707

• The making of America, 1789–1900.

Thematic study

• The people's health, c.1250 to present

• Crime and punishment, c.1250 to present

• Migrants to Britain, c.1250 to present.

Wider world depth study

• The First Crusade, c.1070–1100

• Aztecs and the Spanish conquest, 1519–1535

• Living under Nazi rule, 1933–1945.

British depth study

• The Norman Conquest, 1065–1087

• The Elizabethans, 1580–1603

• London and the Second World War, 1939–45

You also study a 'historic environment'. This could be a historical local site such as a castle or other historic building. You might look at the history of an area during a certain period, for example, London and the Second World War, 1939–45, where you would look at how London was affected, how the people responded to the Blitz and how they lived from day to day.

How you study

There will be lessons covering theory, discussions and debates. You use original sources for research. There may be the opportunity to visit historical sites and museums.

How you are assessed

Assessment is by written exam based on your studies. You also answer questions on the historic environment topic.

What you gain from it

When you study history, you gain an understanding of why things happened; you learn to understand and evaluate written material, to express yourself fluently in written and oral communication and to research, organise and present arguments.

After your GCSEs

Further study

You could progress to history A level where you study British history and different periods of world history. You could consider A level ancient history, studying aspects of the ancient Greek and Roman world. You might also consider related A levels such as politics, sociology, psychology and economics.

History GCSE is useful for other Level 3 qualifications such as BTECs and T levels, as you will have gained excellent communication, research and writing skills.

Apprenticeships and training

History GCSE will be useful for getting into apprenticeships. At Level 3 there are museum and galleries technician and events assistant apprenticeships and at Level 4 there is a historic environment advice assistant apprenticeship. However history GCSE is useful for many other broader apprenticeships. There are a lot to choose from but you could look at apprenticeships in business and administration, retail, library services, travel and tourism and information technology.

Higher/Degree Apprenticeships lead to training as a cultural heritage conservator.

You may need additional qualifications (such as A levels or a BTEC Level 3) to enter Higher or Degree Apprenticeships or you may be able to work up through the apprenticeship route.

Careers

The study of history shows that you have communication and writing skills as well as research skills and an appreciation of the past in Britain and globally. This can be useful in many jobs. Examples of directly-related career areas would be journalism, publishing, libraries and museums, working at historical heritage sites and travel and tourism.

Useful websites

www.bbc.co.uk/bitesize

www.apprenticeships.gov.uk

www.historytoday.com

www.ccskills.org.uk/careers/advice/any/heritage

MATHEMATICS

Maths GCSE helps to build up essential skills that you use every day. This includes doing everyday calculations such as dealing with money or measurements, solving problems, thinking logically and giving attention to detail. You will learn different mathematical techniques and methods on this course. You also learn about decisions and how to choose the best method for solving a maths problem.

Maths is compulsory at Key Stage 4 and can be studied at foundation or higher level. You might study slightly different topics according to the level.

What you study

The topics listed give a broad idea of what you will study. You will need to check with your school or college for the options available to you.

When you study any of these topics you will learn different types of mathematical formulae which are the different techniques for different types of maths calculations. Examples include Pythagoras's theorem and quadratic equations.

- Number, including fractions, decimals, percentages and measurements
- Algebra, including drawing and reading graphs
- Ratio and proportion
- Geometry and measures, including shapes and angles
- Probability
- Statistics, including reading charts and graphs.

How you study

You work on tasks which require you to combine all your skills. Over the course you will be asked to work independently and in groups on a wide variety of activities including solving real-life maths problems.

How you are assessed

The course is assessed by written exams. When you answer the questions, you will need to show your working and how you got the answer. You will need to show that you know the different maths theories that you have learnt during the course.

What you gain from it

Maths teaches you skills that will be useful in everyday life and it is essential for many careers. You might be surprised to learn that maths is a creative subject and you gain investigative and analytical skills and find the best solution to problems.

After your GCSEs

Further study

If you wish to study maths at A level you need to get a good grade in maths GCSE. Maths A level covers pure mathematics, mechanics and statistics. The assessments have a big emphasis on modelling, problem solving and reasoning.

Apprenticeships and training

Maths GCSE will be useful for apprenticeships in many areas including business and finance, engineering, construction, science and research.

Higher/Degree Apprenticeships lead to training in many areas where maths is essential; examples include accountancy, banking, engineering of all types, healthcare, information technology and science.

You may need additional qualifications (such as A levels or a BTEC Level 3) to enter Higher or Degree apprenticeships or you may be able to work up through the apprenticeship route.

Careers

Mathematics is essential for so many careers that it would be difficult to list them all. The analytical, calculation and problem-solving skills you learn in maths can be used in all sorts of jobs at many levels. A bookkeeper will need maths skills as well as the chief executive of a large company; but so will a mechanic, carpet fitter, engineer, astronaut, computer scientist, retail manager and pharmacist. You can see how essential maths is for all careers and daily life. Careers directly related to mathematics include actuary, accountant, maths lecturer or teacher.

Useful websites

www.bbc.co.uk/bitesize

www.apprenticeships.gov.uk

www.ima.org.uk

www.mathscareers.org.uk

MEDIA STUDIES

GCSE in media studies combines practical skills and theory. You learn how the media plays a central role in today's society and culture. You also learn how to challenge the messages everyone is bombarded with from the media and understand that these might not be true. Using your knowledge of the theory and the practical skills you learn, you are able to create your own media product.

What you study

The topics listed give a broad idea of what you will study. You will need to check with your school or college for the options available to you.

You study the different forms of media: television, film, radio, newspapers, magazines, advertising and marketing, online and social media, video games and music videos.

You study some of these in detail and look at how they are constructed and how they work.

• **Media language** – different terms used in media products, how stories are told through different media

• **Media representations** – how different types of people and groups are represented

• **Media industries** – how media industries work, how they are funded and regulated, the different technologies and production techniques used

• **Media audiences** – how different audiences are targeted and reached.

You produce your own media product in response to a set brief. This could be from a wide range of media. Examples might be: a music video, an online or social media product, radio or TV production or a video game.

How you study

You learn some theory and also look at the different types of media but with a critical eye. You examine their structure, how they were created and how they get their point across. You learn practical skills in different types of media, carrying out research and working in groups to complete your project.

How you are assessed

There are written exams on the different types of media you have studied including the forms of media you have studied in depth. Your media product will be assessed and counts towards your final marks.

What you gain from it

Apart from gaining an insight into the real world of the media industry and the technical skills involved, you gain confidence in your critical and analytical skills. You learn communication skills through your written work, as well as research, critical thinking, decision-making and team-working skills.

After your GCSEs

Further study

You could progress to A level media studies or to a Level 3 qualification such as a BTEC in creative digital media production. There is a T level in media, broadcast and production.

Apprenticeships and training

Media studies GCSE will be useful for Level 3 apprenticeships as a broadcast and media systems technical operator, digital marketer, broadcast production assistant and junior content designer. There is a Level 4 apprenticeship as a media production co-ordinator.

Higher/Degree Apprenticeships are available as a broadcast and media systems technician or broadcast and media systems engineer.

You may need additional qualifications (such as A levels or a BTEC Level 3) to enter Higher or Degree Apprenticeships or you may be able to work up through the apprenticeship route.

Careers

This is growing area especially in the areas of e-sports and virtual reality. You may need to gain further qualifications in order to get experience and useful industry contacts and/or you might need to develop a portfolio to help you progress. Job opportunities are in areas like film, photography, publishing, journalism and video game production. There are also many technical careers in media which, for entry, will need further study and training.

Useful websites

www.bbc.co.uk/bitesize

www.apprenticeships.gov.uk

www.bbc.co.uk/careers

www.screenskills.com

www.startintv.com

www.intofilm.org

MODERN FOREIGN LANGUAGES

We live in a multilingual, global society so different languages are all around us. Learning a language can help you understand the life and culture of a country as well as giving you valuable language and communication skills. Neglecting languages in the business world means ignoring potential new markets. You may have the opportunity to use languages for work and they could prove very useful if you are on holiday and need urgent help. Remember not everyone speaks English.

There is a range of languages available at GCSE but the ones most commonly taught are French, German and Spanish. Some schools may offer a wider range including: Arabic, Bengali, Chinese, Italian, Panjabi, Polish, Portuguese, Russian or Urdu. Welsh may also be an option. A GCSE in British Sign Language (BSL) is in development.

Some languages can be studied at foundation or higher level. You might study slightly different topics according to the level. Some schools require students to take a modern foreign language, so check whether a language is part of your options or compulsory.

What you study

The topics listed give a broad idea of what you will study. You will need to check with your school or college for the options available to you.

You develop the main skills of learning a language, and of course you will probably be building on what you already know.

The main language skills are:

• Listening and understanding

• Speaking correctly and confidently

• Reading: a range of styles including advertisements, emails, letters, articles and literary texts, translating texts into English

• Writing: using the correct grammar and vocabulary. Translating texts from the language into English.

As you learn the language, you also learn about the country or countries where the language is spoken and look at different aspects of life which will in turn increase your vocabulary and understanding of the language and people.

Topics you cover could include:

• Family and friends, technology including social media and phones, activities such as music, cinema and sport, customs and festivals of the country, geography, history and social issues

• Different global issues such as the environment, travel and tourism as well as study, career choices and employment in that country

• Different texts and literature which could include poems, letters, short stories, essays, novels or plays from contemporary and historical sources

• Culture of the country or countries where the language is spoken.

How you study

You have formal lessons in grammar and vocabulary and spend time listening to different media, doing role plays and having conversation practice. There will be regular writing and translating tasks, and regular reading and listening exercises. You listen to recordings and watch educational videos which help with language skills and teach you about the culture of the country. There may be the opportunity to visit the country on a study trip or exchange.

How you are assessed

There are written exams based on your listening, reading and writing skills. Your knowledge of the spoken language will be carried out by your school or college and recorded for assessment by an examiner. It usually consists of a role play, a conversation around a photo card and general conversation.

What you gain from it

You gain language skills and an understanding of the culture and history of the country or countries where the language is spoken. The experience of learning a language will help you if you want to learn another language. Your language skills could be of use in employment as well as on holiday. The fact that you can learn a language means that you are an effective communicator with problem-solving and analytical skills. Learning a language also improves your memory.

After your GCSEs

Further study

You could progress to one or more language A levels, where you will study the language, history and culture at a higher level.

Apprenticeships and training

There are many apprenticeships linked to languages at Level 3 and above. Sometimes they will specify a particular language or offer training in further languages. These are in varied career areas such as law, leisure, travel and tourism, retail and education and training. Examples of jobs are legal apprentice, travel consultant, hotel manager and learning support assistant.

Higher/Degree Apprenticeships may also specify particular language skills and again career sectors could range from business to science, engineering and construction.

You may need additional qualifications (such as A levels or a BTEC Level 3) to enter Higher or Degree Apprenticeships or you may be able to work up through the apprenticeship route.

Careers

There are a small number of jobs where languages are the main requirement and examples of these are interpreter, translator and teacher or lecturer. There are other jobs such as working for the Foreign and Commonwealth Office (FCO), in the UK government or MI5 and MI6 who employ foreign language analysts with language skills. For these sorts of jobs a language degree is the usual requirement. Language graduates find employment in many areas such as business, engineering, financial services, media, technology, travel and tourism, and the voluntary and charity sector.

Useful websites

www.bbc.co.uk/bitesize

www.apprenticeships.gov.uk

www.whystudylanguages.ac.uk

www.mi5.gov.uk

www.sis.gov.uk

www.gchq-careers.co.uk

www.gov.uk/government/organisations/foreign-commonwealth-office/about/recruitment

MUSIC

GCSE music involves a range of activities including performing, composing and studying different styles of music from classical music through to music of the present day, including electronic music and DJing which is an option in some schools and colleges. You need to be able to sing or play an instrument to a reasonable standard or have another skill such as DJing. If you do not already play an instrument or sing you must be keen to have lessons.

What you study

The topics listed give a broad idea of what you will study. You will need to check with your school or college for the options available to you.

Understanding music – listening and understanding of musical elements, musical context and musical language. Studying and recognising pieces of music of different types and periods.

There's a wide range of periods and types of music you might study and these include:

• Western classical tradition 1650–1910

• Western classical tradition since 1910

• Music of Broadway 1950s to 1990s

• Rock music of 1960s and 1970s

• Film and computer gaming music 1990s to present

• Pop music 1990s to present.

• Blues music from 1920–1950

• Fusion music incorporating African and/or Caribbean music

• Contemporary British folk music

• British music from Arnold, Britten, Maxwell-Davies and Tavener.

This means you could be studying a Beethoven piano sonata together with songs from Sgt Pepper by the Beatles, or music from the film Little Shop of Horrors, a film soundtrack such as Star Wars or some world music. There is a lot of variety.

Performance – you perfect your performance skills whilst building your knowledge of music theory and different musical styles.

Music technology – technology can play a vital role in both composing and performing music. You might learn to use notation software to create a musical score or use electronic effects or samples in your own compositions.

Composition – learning how to compose and develop musical ideas and how to write them down.

How you study

Lessons are a mixture of theory and practical work. For practical work you will be practising, performing, composing and listening to music. You will receive lessons in your instrument or specialisms in preparation for a solo and group performance exam. You learn music theory, and listening and appraisal skills.

There will be rehearsals that might take place during breaks or after school and also public music performances. You will also attend live music performances.

How you are assessed

Listening – a written exam with listening exercises and written questions using excerpts of music testing both familiar and unfamiliar pieces.

Composition – you compose two pieces of music. One is a free choice and one is linked to a brief set by the exam board. You need to write programme notes for each composition.

Performance – you perform two pieces of music; one as a solo and one as an ensemble with one or more other students. This can include DJing or a production piece using music technology.

What you gain from it

If you are intending to continue studying music or music technology, music GCSE gives you the skills and knowledge to continue your studies. It shows employers you have dedication and commitment to learning a musical instrument and studying music. It also shows you are creative and can work in a team. The confidence that you gain through music will be useful in whatever career you choose.

After your GCSEs

Further study

You could progress to music or music technology A level or consider related qualifications such as a BTEC Nationals in music, music performance or music technology, or the UAL Level 3 Diploma in music performance and production.

Apprenticeships and training

Music GCSE will be useful for apprenticeships at Level 3 as a creative venue technician or live event technician.

Higher/degree Apprenticeships are available in music therapy and creative industries production management.

You may need additional qualifications (such as A levels or a BTEC Level 3) to enter Higher or Degree Apprenticeships or you may be able to work up through the apprenticeship route.

Careers

If you are intending to work in music as a professional musician or composer, you could go to music college or to a university where you could study music on its own or with other subjects. There are separate music colleges known as conservatoires. There are also degrees in performing arts where you study music with other performance subjects like drama and dance.

You don't always need a music degree or diploma for a career in music but it can help as it will give you further performance training and experience and contacts to help you find work. There are lots of other career areas connected with music such music production, studio engineering, music business management, music retail and music therapy.

Useful websites

www.bbc.co.uk/bitesize

www.apprenticeships.gov.uk

www.ukmusic.org/skills-academy/careers-advice

www.getintomusic.org

www.ism.org

www,careersinmusic.co.uk

www.ucas.com/conservatoires

PHYSICAL EDUCATION

Physical education GCSE teaches you the theory of human movement, performance and behaviour in sport and exercise. You learn to analyse and evaluate physical performance (including your own) and apply it to your own experience in different sports. The course allows you to explore a range of activities, both team and individual. You also learn the importance of a healthy, active lifestyle and gain a good knowledge of the anatomy and physiology of the body.

What you study

The topics listed give a broad idea of what you will study. You will need to check with your school or college for the options available to you.

- **Applied anatomy and physiology** – skeletal system, muscular system, cardiovascular and respiratory systems, movement analysis and the effects of exercise on body systems.

- **Physical training** – components of fitness, methods of training, preventing injuries.

- **Performance analysis and evaluation** – the principles of training and their application to personal exercise/training programmes. Use of data: how fitness is measured and analysed, and how such information is used. Measuring your own personal fitness programme.

- **Sports psychology** – understanding the psychological factors that can affect performance in sport such as goal setting, mental preparation, and types of feedback.

- **Socio-cultural influences** – drugs, ethics and violence in sport; media and sponsorship in sport.

- **Health, fitness and wellbeing** – diet and nutrition, physical/emotional and lifestyle choices.

- **Practical performance** – practical performance of three activities including one individual activity such as badminton, tennis, climbing, dance, gymnastics, athletics, swimming or kayaking; and one team activity such as football, netball, handball, rugby or basketball. There is an extensive list of other individual and team sports that can be offered including para sports.

How you study

You study through a mixture of theory and practical lessons. In theory you learn about fitness, health, diet, the skeletal and muscular systems and how the body responds to exercise. In practical lessons you will take part in a range of sports. In order to do well in the practical side of GCSE physical education, you need to be playing sport regularly in lessons, school or college clubs and at clubs outside school or college.

How you are assessed

There are written and practical exams. The practical is an assessment of your top three sports or activities including at least one team sport and one individual activity.

What you gain from it

You learn how to exercise safely and effectively by gaining an understanding of how the body works. This will help you to keep fit. You learn teamwork skills and the ability to work on your own. You also gain skills in recording and analysing data and writing reports.

After your GCSEs

Further study

With a GCSE in physical education you could progress to physical education A level where you will study the subject in depth or to qualifications like BTEC Nationals in sport; sport, fitness and personal training; sports coaching and development; sport and outdoor activities; or sporting excellence and performance.

Apprenticeships and training

Physical education GCSE will be useful for apprenticeships at Level 3 as a community health and sport officer, sports and fitness assistant, sports coach, or sport development professional. There is also an apprenticeship in sporting excellence. The National Schools Apprenticeship scheme offers apprenticeships in schools, with some specialising in sport..

Careers

GCSE physical education is a relevant subject if you are considering playing sport professionally or thinking about careers in sports and active leisure. Examples of these are sports coach, fitness instructor, personal trainer, sports scientist, physiotherapist or teacher. You are likely to need science qualifications for some of these career areas.

Useful websites

www.bbc.co.uk/bitesize

www.apprenticeships.gov.uk

www.skillsactive.com

www.careers-in-sport.co.uk

www.nationalschoolstraining.co.uk/school-apprenticeships

www.healthcareers.nhs.uk

PHYSICS

Physics is all about how the world and the universe works. It covers the study of energy, forces, mechanics, waves, and the structure of atoms. The subject applies to everyday things that we take for granted like phones and the internet, but also stretches out to space and the universe. Physics can lead to many varied and creative careers in areas like engineering, information technology and healthcare.

Sciences are compulsory at Key Stage 4 and can be studied at foundation or higher level. You might study slightly different topics according to the level.

Physics can be studied as a separate subject along with GCSEs in biology and chemistry or as a combined science double award with chemistry and biology.

What you study

Whether you are taking physics GCSE or combined science GCSE, the topics listed give a broad idea of what you will study. You will need to check with your school or college for the options available to you.

• Energy

• Electricity

• Properties of matter

• Atomic structure and radioactivity

• Forces such as gravity and momentum

• Waves, sound and ultrasound, lenses

• Magnetism and electromagnetism – how magnetic fields work

• Space physics – the solar system and the life of a star.

How you study

Although you have to learn about the theories and laws of physics through lessons, practical work forms an important part of the course.

You will do practicals throughout the course to put the theoretical study into practice. These practical experiments help you to plan your work, collect and analyse data, develop your investigational skills and learn to write up the results of your experiments.

How you are assessed

The course is assessed by written exams. They contain a mixture of multiple choice, short answer and extended-response questions. The knowledge and skills gained from practicals is assessed within these exams.

What you gain from it

You learn the important theories and laws of physics and gain an understanding of how they apply to the world. You learn how to plan your work, conduct experiments and analyse data. You gain investigative and analytical skills and develop your communication skills. It is a creative subject as you learn to find the best solution to problems.

After your GCSEs

Further study

If you wish to study sciences further you usually need one or two science subjects at A level or equivalent. Most jobs in physics will require higher level qualifications which you might gain by full-time study or whilst working. Physics-related jobs will also need maths at GCSE or A level.

Apprenticeships and training

Physics GCSE will be useful for apprenticeships as a nuclear health physics monitor, or a laboratory or science manufacturing technician. It will also be useful for apprenticeships in veterinary nursing, animal care, dental technician work or paramedic training.

There are Higher/Degree Apprenticeships in areas such as manufacturing, aerospace, electronic engineering, materials science, the nuclear industry, mechanical and electrical engineering, power engineering, space and rail engineering. They are also available in engineering environmental technologies with specialisms in construction and the built environment and building services engineering. There are also apprenticeships in manufacturing in process development, packaging technology and the food industry.

You may need additional qualifications (such as A levels or a BTEC Level 3) to enter Higher or Degree Apprenticeships or you may be able to work up through the apprenticeship route.

Careers

Physics is essential for many careers and directly-related careers include engineering of all types, including areas such as energy, electronics, medical physics, materials and aerospace.

Physics is also very useful for careers in medicine, pharmacy, forensic science and for research and development work in drugs, pesticides, fuels and food. However the investigative and communication skills you learn in physics can be applied to many other careers including business, finance, information technology and law.

Useful websites

www.bbc.co.uk/bitesize

www.apprenticeships.gov.uk

www.iop.org

www.healthcareers.nhs.uk

PSYCHOLOGY

Psychology is the scientific study of the mind and behaviour. Psychologists carry out experiments and research into why we act the way we do. The study of psychology helps us to understand human behaviour in everyday life. GCSE psychology helps you to develop an understanding of psychological issues and consider how psychology contributes to society.

What you study

The topics listed give a broad idea of what you will study. You will need to check with your school or college for the options available to you.

- **Memory** – the different processes and structures of memory. The factors affecting the accuracy of memory, including interference, context and false memories.

- **Perception** – differences between sensation and perception. The effects of nature and nurture on perception.

- **Cognitive development** – early brain development and the roles of nature and nurture in the brain's growth. The development of intelligence in children.

- **Research methods and data handling** – different ways to investigate behaviour and ways of processing and analysing the data collected.

- **Social influence** – factors affecting conformity and obedience such as the behaviour of crowds.

- **Language, thought and communication** – the development of language and differences between human and animal communication. Different types of non-verbal communication and explanations of how they develop.

- **Brain and neuropsychology** – the nervous system, including the role of the autonomic nervous system in the fight or flight response. How brain scans have been used to examine the functions of different parts of the brain, the effects of brain damage on motor abilities and behaviour.

- **Psychological problems** – mental illness including its effects on the individual and society. This includes studying depression and addiction and how they can be treated.

How you study

There will be formal lessons, discussions, debates, presentations, individual and group work and you will carry out psychological research.

How you are assessed

There are written exams with multiple choice questions, short answer questions and extended-writing questions.

What you gain from it

Learning about how and why people behave in certain ways helps build your understanding of people and your communication skills. You also acquire research and investigative skills. Studying psychology helps you to understand people's behaviour in your daily life.

After your GCSEs

Further study

You could progress to psychology A level where you will study the subject in greater depth.

Apprenticeships and training

Psychology GCSE will be useful for apprenticeships at Level 3 in areas such as business, sales, marketing and also for many health apprenticeships.

A Degree Apprenticeship to train as a clinical associate in psychology is currently in development.

You may need additional qualifications (such as A levels or a BTEC Level 3) to enter Higher or Degree apprenticeships or you may be able to work up through the apprenticeship route.

Careers

If you wish to train as a professional psychologist you will need to study to degree level and then take further qualifications. A knowledge of psychology will be useful for many careers where an understanding of human behaviour is required. People with a psychology background can be found in business, management, medicine, healthcare, teaching, research, marketing, social work, counselling, career guidance, the police and the media.

Useful websites

www.apprenticeships.gov.uk

www.bps.org.uk

www.careersinpsychology.co.uk

www.healthcareers.nhs.uk

RELIGIOUS STUDIES

Religious studies is an important subject for everybody, whether they have a religious faith or not. It is significant in current world affairs and links with many other areas such as music, art, politics, social and cultural issues and even global economics. It covers a wide range of issues that affect millions of people around the world, such as war, abortion, euthanasia and relationships. It helps you to understand the world today and think more deeply about it.

What you study

The topics listed give a broad idea of what you will study. You will need to check with your school or college for the options available to you.

You will study some of the following religions:

• Buddhism

• Christianity or Catholic Christianity

• Hinduism

• Islam

• Judaism

• Sikhism.

For each you study their key beliefs, teachings, holy books and texts, worship and other practices.

Thematic study

You study different themes and how they relate to the religions you have studied.

Examples of themes studied are:

• Relationships and families

• Crime and punishment

• Religion, peace and conflict

• Religion and life

• The existence of God and revelation

• Religion, human rights and social justice.

You look at the ethics and philosophy of the religions you study and learn how the different themes impact and influence the modern world.

How you study

There will be lessons, discussions and debates. There may be the opportunity to visit religious sites and museums.

How you are assessed

Assessment is by written exams based on the religions and topics you have studied. There are written exams with multiple choice questions, short answer questions and extended-writing questions.

What you gain from it

Religious studies GCSE gives you understanding of why things happened in history and politics as they relate to the religions you have studied. You learn to understand and evaluate written material, to express yourself fluently in written and spoken communication and to research, organise and present arguments. It also gives you an understanding of people and how everybody is different.

After your GCSEs

Further study

You could progress to religious studies A level where you study the subject in more detail. You might also consider related A levels such as ancient history or history, and politics, sociology and psychology. Although there are no directly-related Level 3 qualifications, religious studies GCSE could be useful for many BTEC qualifications and T levels as you will have excellent communication, research and writing skills and an understanding of different religions and cultures.

Apprenticeships and training

Religious studies GCSE will be useful for getting into apprenticeships. Although there are no directly-related apprenticeships, religious studies GCSE is useful for many other broader apprenticeships. For example, you could look at apprenticeships in business and administration, caring, retail, library services, travel and tourism and information technology.

Careers

The most relevant careers using religious studies would be minister of religion, lecturer, researcher or teacher. All these will need further study. However, religious studies links to many careers; in fact, anything that involves working alongside people. You will have an understanding of the world and that could be helpful in many job areas such as education, social care, health careers and law.

Useful websites

www.bbc.co.uk/bitesize

www.apprenticeships.gov.uk

www.reonline.org.uk

SOCIOLOGY

GCSE sociology is all about how society works and why. You learn about the structure of society and look at different issues in society through the study of families, education, poverty and crime. You study different theories of sociology and learn and apply various research methods.

What you study

The topics listed give a broad idea of what you will study. You will need to check with your school or college for the options available to you.

- **The sociological approach** – theory about social structures, social processes and social issues.
- **Families** –- what do families do? Is there still a 'normal' family? Have roles in the family changed?
- **Education** – what are schools for? Who does well in school and why? How have policies changed the education system?
- **Crime and deviance** – why do people commit crime? Who is it that commits crime? Can we trust the statistics?
- **Social stratification** – which groups have more power in society? Is this fair? What are the causes of poverty?
- **Research methods in sociology** – theory and design, interpreting data.

How you study

There will be formal lessons, discussions, debates, presentations, individual and group work. You study sociological research and case studies and keep up-to-date with current issues by reading a newspaper or watching TV news.

How you are assessed

There are written exams with multiple choice questions, short answer questions and extended-writing questions.

What you gain from it

You gain a knowledge and perspective of society and social issues and learn to construct logical arguments and draw reasoned conclusions.

You learn how to plan your work, solve problems and analyse different types of data. You gain research and analytical skills and develop your communication skills.

After your GCSEs

Further study

You could progress to sociology A level where you will study the subject in greater depth. You may also want to consider related A level subjects like history, religious studies, psychology, English literature, law and media studies.

Apprenticeships and training

Sociology GCSE will be useful for apprenticeships at Level 3 in housing, healthcare and any job involving research but will also be useful in a wide range of areas such as business, sales, marketing, media and information technology.

Higher/Degree Apprenticeships are available in social work.

You may need additional qualifications (such as A levels or a BTEC Level 3) to enter Higher or Degree apprenticeships or you may be able to work up through the apprenticeship route.

Careers

Sociology GCSE is relevant for a career in a variety of roles involving an understanding of society and research skills. Possible careers include teaching, journalism, social work, healthcare, law, the police, advertising, marketing and local government.

Useful websites

www.bbc.co.uk/bitesize

www.apprenticeships.gov.uk

www.britsoc.co.uk

USEFUL INFORMATION

Joint Council for Qualifications (publish national exam results)
www.jcq.org.uk

EXAM BOARDS

AQA
www.aqa.org.uk

CCEA
www.ccea.org.uk

OCR
www.ocr.org.uk

Pearson
www.pearson.com

WJEC
www.wjec.co.uk

CAREERS AND TRAINING INFORMATION

What do graduates do?
www.luminate.prospects.ac.uk/what-do-graduates-do

Independent and impartial gateway to careers information on the internet
www.careercompanion.co.uk

Careers information aimed at parents and carers
www.parentalguidance.org.uk

Apprenticeships
www.apprenticeships.gov.uk

Higher and Degree Apprenticeships
www.gov.uk/government/publications/higher-and-degree-apprenticeships

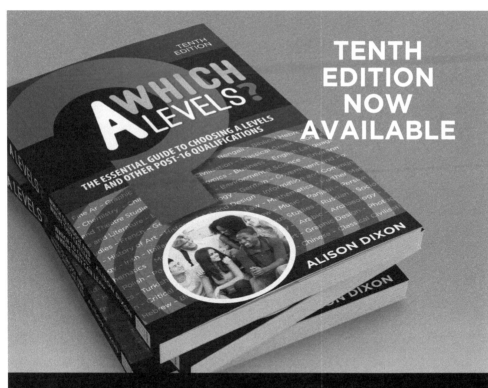

L - #0115 - 060722 - C0 - 234/156/6 - PB - DID3339746